Vegetarian

This edition published in 2011 by Bay Books, an imprint of Murdoch Books Pty Limited

Murdoch Books Australia
Pier 8/9, 23 Hickson Road
Millers Point NSW 2000
Phone: +61 (0)2 8220 2000
Fax: +61 (0)2 8220 2558
www.murdochbooks.com.au

Murdoch Books UK Limited
Erico House, 6th Floor
93–99 Upper Richmond Road
Putney, London SW15 2TG
Phone: +44 (0)20 8785 5995
Fax: +44 (0)20 8785 5985
www.murdochbooks.co.uk

Publisher: Lynn Lewis
Project Manager: Liz Malcolm
Designer: Kylie Mulquin
Editor: Justine Harding
Production: Alexandra Gonzalez

ISBN: 978-0-68134-843-1 (pbk).

Printed in China by Hang Tai Printing Company Limited

IMPORTANT: Those who might be at risk from the effects of salmonella poisoning (the elderly, pregnant women, young children and those suffering from immune deficiency diseases) should consult their doctor with any concerns about eating raw eggs.

OVEN GUIDE: You may find cooking times vary depending on the oven you are using. For fan-forced ovens, as a general rule, set the oven temperature to 20°C (35°F) lower than indicated in the recipe.

Vegetarian

more than 100 fresh, flavoursome recipes

bay books

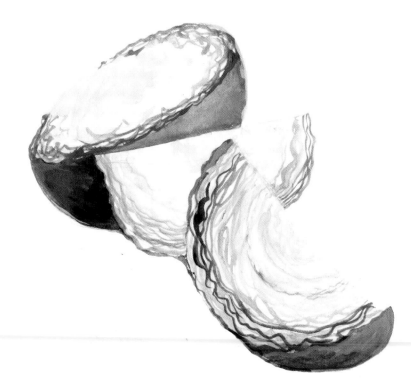

Contents

The vegetarian food pyramid

It is just as possible to have a poor diet eating exclusively vegetarian foods as it is eating excessive animal products. The vegetarian food pyramid is a good starting point if you want to check whether your current diet is adequate. Its underlying principle is simple: it shows food groups in the form of a pyramid, with those that should comprise the bulk of your diet forming the base of the pyramid, and those to be consumed more sparingly at the top.

Eat most

- Grains: wheat, rice, barley, corn, oats, rye, millet, buckwheat
- Foods made from grains: pasta, bread, wholegrain breakfast cereals
- Fruit and vegetables

Eat moderately

- Dairy: milk, yoghurt, cheese
- Pulses: peas, beans of all kinds, lentils
- Nuts
- Eggs

Eat least

- Sugar, honey, sweets
- Butter, cream, margarine, oils
- Alcohol, tea, coffee

Navigating the food maze

Meal planning becomes easier if you make a habit of using the food pyramid as a guide. Your daily diet should be stacked with the staple foods from the 'eat most' group: fruit, cereals and toast for breakfast; bread or bread rolls, salads or cooked vegetable dishes and fruit for lunch; pasta or rice-based main course for dinner with fresh bread or rolls, and more fruit for dessert or snacks.

Small amounts of dairy foods from the 'eat moderately' group can be part of the day's meals (unless you are a vegan): yoghurt with breakfast or lunch, a little cheese with lunch or dinner. Dinner can include filling dishes and hearty soups made from dried beans or lentils, as well as tasty egg dishes. Nuts are great for snacking.

The 'eat least' category means exactly that—a small amount of butter or margarine on your breakfast toast, a little virgin olive oil with your salad or to stir-fry the onions for the evening meal, the occasional glass of wine with dinner. A sugary treat is fine if it isn't a regular occurrence, and tea and coffee can be enjoyed in moderation. You can balance the nutritional content of the day's meals so that the overall pattern satisfies the food pyramid guidelines. Compensate for an unavoidably fatty lunch, for example, with an evening meal made up of vegetables, grains and fruit.

Eating out can be a trap, so keep the food pyramid in mind when ordering food and to compensate for any imbalances when preparing food for yourself at home.

Easy does it

Changing the habits of a lifetime is not something we can do overnight. If your usual diet doesn't bear much resemblance to the food pyramid, you can move gradually towards a healthier way of eating. Don't worry if every meal is not perfectly balanced. You can correct the proportions over the course of each week as you adjust to buying and cooking healthier foods and experiment with new dishes. Replace refined foods with whole foods, and high-fat dairy products with reduced-fat versions. Check labels for salt, sugar and fat content, and for food additives. Have fun making your own versions of soups, sauces and even breakfast cereals, rather than buying the ready-made product. This way you can control what goes into your body.

Children generally enjoy healthy eating. Pastas, fruit, yoghurt, peanut butter, cheese, milk and nuts are usually popular. The difficulties only arise if you are trying to change bad habits: doing it gradually is best.

Menu planning

Aim to shop and eat for health, using the food pyramid as a guide. Buy several different kinds of rice, couscous, a variety of pastas, lots of breads (freeze loaves and flatbreads if you have room), breakfast cereals and interesting flours.

Replenish your store of fresh produce regularly, but do it systematically. Shop with some idea of your meal plans from week to week to avoid wastage. Taking advantage of enticing seasonal produce by buying up big is pointless if fruit and vegetables languish at the bottom of your refrigerator while you think of a way to use them. Vary your choices as much as possible to keep your diet interesting and to maximise the nutritional benefits.

Buy cheeses, milk, yoghurt and eggs regularly, but plan how much you are likely to need to avoid overloading on dietary fat.

Tinned foods are an essential pantry item: tinned beans of every variety are great time-savers if you don't want to soak and cook your own. Tomato pastes and tinned tomatoes are invaluable; also keep olive oils—extra virgin for flavour, lighter grades for cooking—on hand. Bottled sauces such as pesto, basic pasta sauces and chilli sauce are versatile flavour enhancers.

A feast of flavours

One of the great joys of vegetarian eating lies in its versatility. It's an opportunity to take exotic detours through some of the world's most wonderful cuisines, broadening your menu options and expanding your cooking skills. The limitations of the traditional meat-and-two-veg diet will soon become obvious!

Many cultures feature a strong vegetarian component and some are exclusively vegetarian, having evolved this way of eating for economic as well as religious reasons. These cuisines are the source of delicious, nutritious dishes that any cook can easily master. From Mexico, we get tortillas and beans; from the Orient, tofu, tempeh and rice; from the Middle East, hummus with lavash or pitta bread; from North Africa and the Mediterranean, couscous and chickpeas.

When you don't have to make meat, chicken or fish the centrepiece of your meals, mealtimes become much more interesting and it becomes much easier to serve food buffet-style. Many ethnic cuisines actually demand this way of serving and eating, offering platters of complementary dishes from which people help themselves, adding accompaniments of their choice.

With vegetarian food you can break all the rules. You can serve first courses as main courses, mains as starters, or make a soup the star of your meal. Many exotic vegetarian dishes can be served as either a side dish, main course, light meal or snack.

All you need is a little knowledge, a few interesting ingredients, and some thought about complementary flavours and textures. You will then discover that it is really quite impossible to be bored by vegetarian food!

Wake up your tastebuds

The incomparable flavours of fresh whole foods can be enhanced with spices and condiments such as harissa, chilli powders and pastes, and curry spice mixtures. Herbs are also indispensable, while pickles, chutneys, sauces, mustards and relishes can be used to dress up any number of dishes.

Certain herbs and spices go particularly well with certain foods:

- basil with tomatoes and cheeses
- cinnamon, cardamom and cloves with yoghurt, cream and milk dishes
- chives in soups, dips, salads, sandwiches and sauces, and with eggs, potatoes and cheese
- dill in salads, egg dishes and with potatoes
- chopped herbs with pasta and rice dishes
- ginger with carrots
- lemongrass in rice dishes and Asian-style sauces
- lemon thyme in salads and with cooked vegetables
- oregano and marjoram with eggs, in salads and marinades, and with cauliflower and tomatoes
- mint with potatoes, rice and in tabouleh
- paprika with eggs, cheeses and in casseroles
- parsley in salads and with tomatoes
- rosemary with eggplant (aubergine), tomatoes and zucchini (courgette)
- sage in bean, cheese and egg dishes
- garlic is brilliant with just about anything savoury
- cloves with oranges

Consider colour and texture as well as taste and nutritional value. Serve a pasta bake with a salad or crisp-textured greens such as asparagus or snow peas (mangetout) to lend extra colour and crunch. Make simple vegetable dishes and salads more interesting and nutritious by sprinkling them with chopped nuts or seeds—try a mixture of pepitas (pumpkin seeds) and sesame seeds tossed in soy sauce and roasted in the oven (it will keep for months in the refrigerator in an airtight jar). Include lots of interesting breads when serving vegetarian foods, including flatbreads such as lavash, chapattis, rotis, poppadoms, tortillas and pitta.

Stock up the pantry before you begin to roam through the varied world of vegetarian cookery. This will ensure you will always have the necessary ingredients for a successful dish and you won't need to compromise on flavour. Most supermarkets stock a huge variety of the items you will need, but don't forget to explore delicatessens, food markets and Asian and other ethnic food stores for condiments and more unusual ingredients.

The recipes in this book are grouped into basic chapters, from which you can browse and plunder at will. Enjoy experimenting and giving recipes your own individual twist. We hope this book inspires you on your gastronomic journey through some of the world's great vegetarian cuisines!

Introduction

Snacks & small bites

Each of these recipes is delicious
served solo, but you can easily build up
a selection into a full-scale meal.

SYRIAN LENTIL PIZZAS

preparation time 45 minutes plus 1 hour proving
cooking time 1 hour
serves 6

90 g (3 oz/½ cup) brown lentils
60 ml (2 fl oz/¼ cup) olive oil, plus
    extra, for drizzling
4 brown onions, chopped
50 g (2 oz/⅓ cup) pine nuts
½ teaspoon ground cinnamon
1 teaspoon ground allspice
3 ripe tomatoes, seeded and finely
    chopped
125 g (4½ oz/1 cup) crumbled feta
    cheese
1 tablespoon pomegranate molasses
2 lemons, cut into wedges

PIZZA DOUGH
225 g (8 oz/1½ cups) plain
    (all-purpose) flour
225 g (8 oz/1½ cups) wholemeal
    (whole-wheat) flour
2 teaspoons dried yeast
2 teaspoons salt
½ teaspoon sugar
2 tablespoons olive oil

● To make the pizza dough, combine the plain and wholemeal flours, yeast, salt and sugar in a large bowl. Make a well in the centre. Combine the oil with 310 ml (10¾ fl oz/1¼ cups) lukewarm water. Add to the flour mixture and mix until a soft dough forms, adding another tablespoon of lukewarm water if necessary. Turn out onto a lightly floured surface and knead for 8–10 minutes, or until smooth and elastic. Place in an oiled bowl, turning to coat in the oil. Cover with plastic wrap and stand in a warm, draught-free place for 1 hour, or until doubled in size.

● Meanwhile, place the lentils in a saucepan with 750 ml (26 fl oz/3 cups) cold water and bring to the boil over high heat. Reduce the heat to low, cover and simmer for 30 minutes, or until the lentils are very tender. Drain well.

- Heat the olive oil in a non-stick frying pan over medium heat. Add the onion and cook, stirring, for 10 minutes, or until softened and light golden. Stir in the pine nuts, cinnamon and allspice and cook for 1 minute. Remove from the heat, then stir in the lentils, tomato, feta and pomegranate molasses. Season to taste with sea salt and freshly ground black pepper.

- Preheat the oven to 200°C (400°F/Gas 6). Line two baking trays with baking paper. Knock down the pizza dough, then break off pieces the size of a golf ball (about 45 g/1½ oz each). Roll each one out on a lightly floured surface until 3 mm (⅛ inch) thick and about 12 cm (4½ inches) in diameter. Place the rounds on the baking trays and bake for 5 minutes. Remove from the oven and pierce several times with a fork to deflate.

- Spread about 70 g (2½ oz/⅓ cup) of the lentil mixture over each round, leaving a 2 cm (¾ inch) border. Drizzle with a little extra olive oil and bake for 10–12 minutes, or until the bases are golden brown around the edges and cooked through.

- Serve immediately, with the lemon wedges.

CARROT DUMPLINGS WITH DILL SOUR CREAM

preparation time 45 minutes plus 20 minutes soaking
cooking time 50 minutes
makes 24

60 ml (2 fl oz/¼ cup) olive oil
1 brown onion, finely chopped
2 garlic cloves, crushed
4 carrots (about 400 g/14 oz),
   coarsely grated
2 hard-boiled eggs, peeled and finely
   chopped
125 g (4½ oz/½ cup) cottage cheese
2 tablespoons finely chopped flat-leaf
   (Italian) parsley, plus extra leaves,
   to garnish
1 tablespoon finely chopped dill,
   plus extra sprigs, to garnish
1 tablespoon snipped chives,
   plus extra lengths, to garnish
30 g (1 oz) butter

DUMPLINGS
350 g (12 oz/2⅓ cups) plain
   (all-purpose) flour, plus extra,
   for dusting
2 eggs, lightly whisked
100 g (3½ oz) sour cream

DILL SOUR CREAM
100 g (3½ oz) sour cream
2 tablespoons finely chopped dill
1 tablespoon snipped chives
2 teaspoons lemon juice

- To make the dumplings, place the flour in a large bowl. Mix together the eggs, sour cream and 60 ml (2 fl oz/¼ cup) water. Add to the flour and mix with a wooden spoon, gradually adding another 90 ml (3 fl oz) water until a slightly soft dough forms. Turn out onto a lightly floured surface and knead gently for 3–4 minutes until smooth, adding a little extra flour if the dough is sticky. Dust lightly with flour, cover with plastic wrap and refrigerate for 20 minutes.

- Meanwhile, heat 1 tablespoon of the olive oil in a frying pan over medium–low heat. Add the onion and cook, stirring, for 8 minutes, or until softened. Add the garlic and carrot and cook for another 5 minutes, or until the carrot is tender. Transfer the mixture to a bowl, then gently stir in the egg, cottage cheese and herbs. Season to taste with sea salt and freshly ground black pepper and set aside.

- Divide the dough in half. Roll one portion on a floured surface until 2 mm (¹⁄₁₆ inch) thick, using a little extra flour if the dough is sticky. Cut the dough into rounds using a 9 cm (3½ inch) cutter. Place 1 tablespoon of the carrot mixture on one half of each round. Brush the edges with water, fold the dough over to enclose the filling, then pinch the edges firmly to seal. Repeat with the remaining dough and carrot mixture.

- Bring a large saucepan of water to the boil. Cook the dumplings, about 12 at a time, for 3–4 minutes, or until tender. Drain well.

- Heat the remaining olive oil in a heavy-based non-stick frying pan over medium–high heat. Add the butter and heat until foaming. Cook the pierogi in batches for 1 minute on each side, or until golden.

- To make the dill sour cream, combine the sour cream, dill and chives in a small serving bowl. Stir in the lemon juice and season to taste.

- Serve the dumplings scattered with extra parsley dill and chives, with the dill sour cream.

CRISPY CHEESE AND CURRY LENTIL BALLS

preparation time 15 minutes
cooking time 20 minutes
makes about 30

250 g (9 oz/1 cup) red lentils
4 spring onions (scallions)
1 large zucchini (courgette)
2 garlic cloves, crushed
1 teaspoon ground cumin

80 g (3 oz/1 cup) fresh breadcrumbs
125 g (4½ oz/1 cup) grated cheddar
cheese
150 g (5½ oz/1 cup) polenta
oil, for deep-frying

● Put the lentils in a saucepan and cover with water. Bring to the boil, reduce the heat, cover and simmer for 10 minutes, or until tender. Drain.

● Meanwhile, chop the spring onion and grate the zucchini.

● Combine half the lentils in a food processor or blender with the spring onion and garlic. Process until smooth. Transfer to a large bowl, then stir in the remaining lentils, cumin, breadcrumbs, cheese and zucchini until well combined. Roll level teaspoons of the mixture into balls and toss lightly in the polenta to coat.

● Fill a heavy-based saucepan one-third full of oil and heat the oil to 180°C (350°F), or until a cube of bread dropped into the oil browns in 15 seconds. Cook small batches of the lentil balls in the oil for 1 minute each batch, or until golden brown, crisp and heated through. Carefully remove with tongs or a slotted spoon and drain on crumpled paper towel. Serve hot.

POTATO AND CASHEW SAMOSAS

preparation time 20 minutes
cooking time 40 minutes
makes 16

3 all-purpose potatoes
1 tablespoon olive oil
2 teaspoons chopped ginger
90 g (3 oz) roasted cashew nuts,
    chopped
15 g (½ oz/¼ cup) shredded coconut

60 ml (2 fl oz/¼ cup) coconut cream
3 tablespoons chopped coriander
    (cilantro) leaves
4 sheets shortcrust (pie) pastry
oil, for deep-frying

● Finely dice the potatoes. Heat the oil in a large heavy-based frying pan and cook the potatoes and ginger for 8 minutes over medium heat, stirring constantly. Add the cashews, shredded coconut, coconut cream and coriander, stir to combine and season. Leave to cool.

● Cut each pastry sheet into four. Place quarter cupfuls of the filling in the centre of each square, then brush the edges of the pastry with water. Press the edges of the pastry together, twist to seal, then chill for 15 minutes.

● Fill a large heavy-based saucepan one-third full of oil and heat the oil to 180°C (350°F), or until a cube of bread dropped into the oil browns in 15 seconds. Deep-fry the samosas in batches for 6 minutes, or until golden and crisp. Drain on paper towel and serve immediately with a dip made from plain yoghurt, finely chopped cucumber, chopped chilli and perhaps some chopped mint, if desired.

VIETNAMESE RICE PAPER ROLLS

preparation time 45 minutes
cooking time 20 minutes
makes 34

3 eggs, lightly beaten
1½ tablespoons peanut oil
200 g (7 oz) firm tofu, drained and
cut into 5 mm (¼ inch)-thick slices
2 red Asian shallots, finely diced
2 tablespoons soy sauce
500 g (1 lb 2 oz) jicama or Jerusalem
artichokes, peeled and grated,
excess liquid removed (see Note)
2 carrots, coarsely grated
100 g (3½ oz) bean sprouts, tails
trimmed

60 ml (2 fl oz/¼ cup) hoisin sauce,
plus extra, to serve
2 teaspoons chilli sauce
4 spring onions (scallions), cut into
thin strips about 4 cm (1½ inches)
long
1 bunch Vietnamese mint, leaves
picked
50 g (2 oz/⅓ cup) roasted peanuts,
chopped, plus extra, to serve
34 rice paper wrappers, about 22 cm
(8½ inches) in diameter

● Whisk the eggs in a small bowl, then season with sea salt and freshly ground black pepper.

● Heat 1 teaspoon of the oil in a small non-stick frying pan over medium heat. Add half the egg mixture, swirling to create a thin omelette. Cook for 2 minutes, or until the egg has just set, then transfer to a plate. Repeat with the remaining egg, adding a little more oil to the pan as needed. Allow the omelettes to cool, then roll them up and cut them crossways, to form thin strips. Set aside.

● Heat another 2 teaspoons of the oil in a larger non-stick frying pan over high heat. Add the tofu slices and cook for 2 minutes on each side, or until lightly browned. Remove from the pan and allow to cool, then cut into thin strips. Set aside.

- Wipe the pan clean and heat the remaining oil over medium heat. Add the shallot and cook, stirring, for 2 minutes. Add the soy sauce, jicama and carrot, and cook, uncovered, for 6−8 minutes, or until the vegetables are tender, stirring often. Transfer to a bowl and allow to cool. Season to taste, add the bean sprouts and stir to combine.

- Combine the hoisin and chilli sauce in a small bowl. Place the sauce, egg strips, tofu, jicama mixture, spring onion, mint and peanuts in neat piles on a clean work surface.

- Place one rice paper round in a bowl of lukewarm water for 10 seconds, or until soft and pliable. Remove from the water and place on a clean tea towel (dish towel). Spread a small amount of the hoisin mixture in the centre of the round, then add a small amount of the omelette, tofu, 1 tablespoon of the jicama mixture, a strip of spring onion, one mint leaf and a sprinkle of peanuts. Fold in each side of the rice paper, then roll up firmly to enclose the filling. Repeat with the remaining rice paper wrappers and filling.

- Serve immediately with the extra hoisin sauce sprinkled with the extra peanuts.

Note Jicama is sometimes know as yam bean. It is a tuber with a crunchy texture and mild flavour. To remove the excess liquid, squeeze the grated flesh between your hands.

Snacks & small bites

SPRING ROLLS

preparation time 45 minutes
cooking time 20 minutes
makes 20

4 dried Chinese mushrooms
150 g (5½ oz) fried tofu
1 large carrot
70 g (2½ oz) water chestnuts
6 spring onions (scallions)
150 g (5½ oz) Chinese cabbage
   (wong bok)

1 tablespoon oil
2 garlic cloves, crushed
1 tablespoon grated fresh ginger
1 tablespoon soy sauce
white pepper, to taste
1 tablespoon cornflour (cornstarch)
10 large spring roll wrappers
oil, extra, for deep-frying

• Soak the dried mushrooms in boiling water for 20 minutes. Drain and squeeze to remove any excess liquid. Slice the mushroom caps and discard the hard stems.

• Cut the tofu into fine strips and cut the carrot into very fine batons. Chop the water chestnuts and spring onions and shred the Chinese cabbage.

• Heat the oil in a large wok, swirling gently to coat the base and side. Stir-fry the garlic, ginger, tofu, carrot and water chestnuts for 30 seconds, over high heat. Add the spring onion and Chinese cabbage and cook for 1 minute, or until the cabbage is just softened. Add the soy sauce and some salt, white pepper and sugar, to taste, then allow to cool. Add the sliced mushroom caps.

• Mix the cornflour with 2 tablespoons water to form a paste. Keep the spring roll wrappers covered with a clean damp tea towel (dish towel) while you work. Place two wrappers on a board, one on top of the other. (The rolls are made with two layers of wrappers.) Cut the large square into four squares. Brush the edges of each square with a little cornflour paste. Place about 1 tablespoon of the filling in the centre of one square. With a corner facing you, roll up the wrapper firmly, folding in the sides as you roll. Repeat with the remaining wrappers and filling.

• Fill a deep heavy-based saucepan one-third full of oil and heat the oil to 180°C (350°F), or until a cube of bread dropped into the oil browns in 15 seconds. Deep-fry the spring rolls, about four at a time, for 3 minutes, or until golden. Drain on crumpled paper towel.

STUFFED VINE LEAVES WITH EGG AND LEMON SAUCE

preparation time 35 minutes plus 30 minutes soaking
cooking time 1 hour
makes about 20

100 g (3½ oz/½ cup) long-grain white rice

400 g (14 oz) tin chickpeas, rinsed and drained well

1 ripe tomato, peeled and chopped

1 brown onion, finely chopped

2 garlic cloves, finely chopped

3 tablespoons chopped flat-leaf (Italian) parsley

1½ tablespoons chopped dill

1 teaspoon ground cinnamon

2 tablespoons tomato paste (concentrated purée)

225 g (8 oz) vine leaves in brine, rinsed and dried

2 tablespoons lemon juice

EGG AND LEMON SAUCE

375 ml (13 fl oz/1½ cups) vegetable stock

80 ml (2½ fl oz/⅓ cup) lemon juice, plus extra, to taste

2 teaspoons finely grated lemon rind

6 large egg yolks

● Place the rice in a bowl, pour enough boiling water over to cover, then leave to soak for 30 minutes. Drain well.

● Mash the chickpeas in a bowl using a fork. Add the rice, tomato, onion, garlic, herbs, cinnamon and tomato paste and mix until well combined.

- Use about five vine leaves to line the base of a large saucepan (this will prevent the stuffed vine leaves from sticking to the pan). Lay another vine leaf on a clean work surface and place 1 tablespoon of the rice mixture across the centre, near the stem end. Fold the sides of the vine leaf over the filling, then roll the vine leaf into a cigar shape. Repeat with the remaining leaves and filling.

- Place the stuffed leaves in the lined saucepan, packing them in tight layers. Add the lemon juice and about 350 ml (12 fl oz) water, or enough to cover the leaves. Place a small plate directly over the stuffed leaves to keep them immersed in the liquid, then cover the saucepan with a lid. Bring the liquid to a simmer, then cook over low heat for 1 hour, adding a little extra water as necessary to stop the leaves cooking dry.

- Meanwhile, make the egg and lemon sauce. Heat the stock, lemon juice and lemon rind in a small saucepan until just boiling; remove from the heat. Lightly beat the egg yolks in a bowl, then pour some of the hot liquid over them and stir until well combined. Pour the egg mixture into the hot stock mixture and cook over medium–low heat, stirring constantly with a wooden spoon, for 15–20 minutes, or until the sauce has thickened slightly (do not simmer). Taste and stir in extra lemon juice if needed.

- Serve the vine leaves warm, with the warm egg and lemon sauce.

VEGETARIAN DOLMADES

preparation time 1 hour
cooking time 1 hour 15 minutes
makes about 50

6 spring onions (scallions)
125 ml (4 fl oz/½ cup) olive oil
150 g (5½ oz/¾ cup) long-grain rice
15 g (½ oz) chopped mint
2 tablespoons chopped dill
170 ml (5½ fl oz/⅔ cup) lemon juice

35 g (1 oz/¼ cup) currants
40 g (1½ oz/¼ cup) pine nuts
235 g (8½ oz) packaged vine leaves
  (about 50)
2 tablespoons olive oil, extra

● Chop the spring onions. Heat the oil in a saucepan. Add the spring onion and cook over medium heat for 1 minute. Stir in the rice, mint, dill and half the lemon juice. Season to taste. Add 250 ml (9 fl oz/1 cup) water and bring to the boil, then reduce the heat, cover and simmer for 20 minutes. Remove the lid, fork through the currants and pine nuts, cover with a paper towel, then the lid and leave to cool.

● Rinse the vine leaves and gently separate. Drain, then dry on paper towel. Trim any thick stems with scissors.

● Line the base of a 20 cm (8 inch) saucepan with any torn or misshapen leaves. Choose the larger leaves for filling and use the smaller leaves to patch up any gaps. Place a leaf, shiny side down. Spoon a tablespoon of filling into the centre, bring in the sides and roll up tightly from the stem end. Place, seam side down, with the stem end closest to you, in the base of the pan, arranging them close together in a single layer.

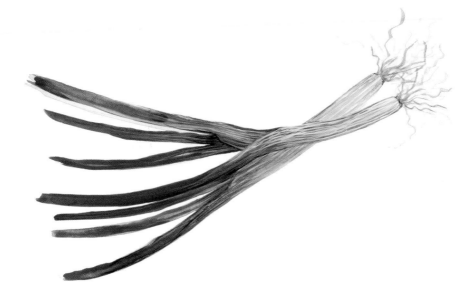

● Pour in the rest of the lemon juice, the extra oil and about 185 ml (6 fl oz/ ¾ cup) water to just cover the dolmades. Cover with an inverted plate and place a tin on the plate to firmly compress the dolmades and keep them in place while they are cooking. Cover with the lid.

● Bring to the boil, then reduce the heat and simmer for 45 minutes. Cool in the pan. Serve at room temperature.

CARAMEL TOFU WITH PEANUTS AND GINGER

preparation time 15 minutes
cooking time 15 minutes
serves 4

175 g (6 oz) firm tofu

2 tablespoons caster (superfine) sugar

1 tablespoon soy sauce

1 cm (½ inch) piece ginger, finely grated

1 cm (½ inch) piece galangal, finely grated (optional)

1 small garlic clove, very thinly sliced

½ star anise

steamed bok choy (pak choy)

few sprigs of coriander (cilantro)

1½ tablespoons blanched roasted peanuts and steamed rice, to serve

- Cut the tofu into 3 cm (1¼ inch) cubes, then set aside.

- Combine the sugar and 2 tablespoons water in a small frying pan over medium heat. Cook the mixture, shaking the pan occasionally, for 5 minutes or until it is a deep caramel colour. Working quickly and taking care as the mixture will spit, remove the pan from the heat, then add 80 ml (2½ fl oz/⅓ cup) water, the soy sauce, ginger, galangal, if using, garlic and star anise. Return the pan to the heat and cook over a medium–low heat for 1 minute or until it boils gently and is smooth.

- Add the tofu to the pan and cook for 5–6 minutes, turning once, or until the tofu is a deep caramel colour and heated through, and the liquid has reduced. Remove the star anise. Place the tofu in a serving bowl with the bok choy, spoon the sauce over, scatter with the coriander and serve with the peanuts and steamed rice on the side

TOFU SKEWERS WITH PEANUT SAUCE

preparation time 15 minutes plus 2 hours marinating
cooking time 15 minutes
makes 24

2 tablespoons kecap manis
2 tablespoons soy sauce
4 garlic cloves, crushed
1 teaspoon grated fresh ginger
1 tablespoon peanut oil
2 teaspoons ground cumin
2 teaspoons ground coriander
2 teaspoons sweet chilli sauce
700 g (1 lb 9 oz) firm tofu, drained
    and cut into 2 cm (¾ inch) chunks
500 g (1 lb 2 oz) cherry tomatoes,
    halved
steamed brown rice, to serve

PEANUT SAUCE
1 teaspoon peanut oil
2 garlic cloves, crushed
250 g (9 oz/1 cup) crunchy peanut
    butter
2 tablespoons soy sauce
125 ml (4 fl oz/½ cup) coconut milk

• Combine the kecap manis, soy sauce, garlic, ginger, peanut oil, cumin, coriander and sweet chilli sauce in a bowl and stir to combine. Reserve 2 tablespoons of the marinade for the peanut sauce.

• Add the tofu to the bowl and gently toss to coat. Cover and marinate in the refrigerator for 2 hours. Meanwhile, soak 24 wooden skewers in cold water for 30 minutes to prevent scorching.

• To make the peanut sauce, heat the peanut oil in a small saucepan over low heat. Add the garlic and sauté for 2 minutes, then add the peanut butter, soy sauce, coconut milk, reserved marinade and 125 ml (4 fl oz/½ cup) water. Stir well, then heat slowly until hot.

● Preheat the grill (broiler) to medium. Remove the tofu from the marinade and drain well, reserving the marinade for basting. Thread the tofu chunks and cherry tomato halves onto each skewer.

● Grill (broil) the skewers for 4 minutes on each side, or until browned, basting with the reserved marinade and turning during cooking. Serve with the remaining peanut sauce and steamed brown rice.

STUFFED TOMATOES WITH BAKED YOGHURT

preparation time 15 minutes
cooking time 35 minutes
serves 6

12 large, firm vine-ripened or organic
    tomatoes (about 1.8 kg/4 lb), with
    stems on
olive oil, for drizzling

COUSCOUS STUFFING

125 g (4½ oz/⅔ cup) instant couscous
125 ml (4 fl oz/½ cup) vegetable
    stock
4 garlic cloves, finely chopped
1 tablespoon olive oil
100 g (3½ oz/⅔ cup) crumbled feta
    cheese
75 g (2½ oz) pitted green olives,
    chopped
400 g (14 oz) tin chickpeas, rinsed
    and drained
3 tablespoons chopped mint leaves
3 tablespoons chopped flat-leaf
    (Italian) parsley

BAKED YOGHURT

500 g (1 lb 2 oz/2 cups) Greek-style
    yoghurt
1 garlic clove, crushed
1 teaspoon oregano
2 eggs, plus 2 egg yolks
65 g (2½ oz/½ cup) crumbled feta
    cheese
2 tablespoons finely chopped flat-leaf
    (Italian) parsley

- Preheat the oven to 180°C (350°F/Gas 4). Using a serrated knife, carefully cut off the top of each tomato in one piece to make a lid about 1 cm (½ inch) thick. Using a teaspoon, gently remove the seeds from inside the tomato and the tomato top, and scoop out the flesh, leaving a firm shell. Reserve the seeds and any juice for another use; dice the scooped-out tomato flesh and reserve.

- To make the couscous stuffing, place the couscous in a large heatproof bowl and bring the stock to the boil in a small saucepan. Pour the hot stock over the couscous, then cover and leave to stand for 3 minutes. Fluff the couscous with a fork.

- Add the reserved tomato flesh and the remaining stuffing ingredients and mix well. Season to taste with sea salt and freshly ground black pepper.

- Spoon the couscous stuffing into each tomato and replace the lids. Place the tomatoes in a baking dish and drizzle with olive oil; set aside.

- For the baked yoghurt, place the yoghurt, garlic and oregano in a small saucepan over low heat and gently stir until hot — do not allow to boil. Remove from the heat and keep warm. In a small bowl, lightly beat the eggs and egg yolks and season to taste. Slowly pour the heated yoghurt into the eggs, whisking continuously until combined. Stir in the feta and parsley.

- Pour the mixture into six 125 ml (4 fl oz/½ cup) ramekins. Place the ramekins in a deep baking dish and pour enough boiling water into the baking dish to come halfway up the side of the ramekins.

- Transfer the yoghurt and tomato baking dishes to the oven, keeping them both uncovered. Bake the yoghurt for 30 minutes, or until set; remove the ramekins from the baking dish and stand for 5 minutes. Bake the tomatoes for a further 5 minutes, or until the filling is heated through.

- Serve the tomatoes with the baked yoghurt.

STUFFED ZUCCHINI WITH YOGHURT AND SPICED TOMATO SAUCE

preparation time 30 minutes
cooking time 1 hour 20 minutes
serves 4

12 Lebanese zucchini (courgettes), measuring 12–15 cm (4½–6 inches) in length (see Note)
150 g (5½ oz/¾ cup) long-grain white rice
2 tablespoons olive oil
1 large brown onion, finely chopped
1 tablespoon pine nuts
3 tablespoons finely chopped flat-leaf (Italian) parsley, plus extra, to garnish
3 tablespoons finely chopped mint leaves, plus extra, to garnish
½ teaspoon ground cinnamon
½ teaspoon ground allspice
200 g (7 oz/1⅓ cups) feta cheese, crumbled
halved cherry tomatoes, to serve

CUMIN-SPICED TOMATO SAUCE

1 tablespoon olive oil
1 brown onion, finely chopped
2 garlic cloves, crushed
60 g (2 oz/¼ cup) tomato paste (concentrated purée)
2½ teaspoons ground cumin
1 dried bay leaf
400 g (14 oz) tin chopped tomatoes
375 ml (13 fl oz/1½ cups) vegetable stock

MINTED YOGHURT

250 g (9 oz/1 cup) Greek-style yoghurt
1 garlic clove, crushed with a little sea salt
1 tablespoon chopped mint leaves

- To make the cumin-spiced tomato sauce, heat the olive oil in a saucepan over medium heat. Cook the onion, stirring, for 5–8 minutes, or until softened. Stir in the garlic, tomato paste and cumin and cook, stirring, for 2 minutes. Add the remaining ingredients and stir to combine well. Bring to the boil, remove from the heat and set aside.

- Combine the minted yoghurt ingredients in a small bowl. Mix well, then cover and refrigerate until required.

- Preheat the oven to 180°C (350°F/Gas 4). Trim about 1 cm (½ inch) from each end of the zucchini. Using an apple corer or a narrow sharp knife and a teaspoon, carefully cut out the flesh from the centre of each zucchini, leaving at least a 5 mm (¼ inch)-thick shell all around. Reserve the removed flesh.

- Wash the rice until the water runs clear, then drain well and set aside. Heat the olive oil in a frying pan over medium heat. Cook the onion, stirring, for 5–8 minutes, or until softened. Add the pine nuts and cook for a further 2 minutes, stirring occasionally. Tip the mixture into a bowl, then stir in the rice, herbs, spices and feta until well combined. Season to taste with sea salt and freshly ground black pepper.

- Fill the hollowed-out zucchini with the rice stuffing until three-quarters filled. Use the reserved flesh as a cork to plug the ends of each zucchini. Spoon one-third of the tomato sauce over the base of a baking dish just large enough to hold the zucchini snugly. Place the zucchini side by side over the sauce, then pour the remaining sauce over the top. Seal the baking dish with foil. Bake for 1 hour, or until the rice and zucchini are tender.

- Serve the zucchini warm or hot, drizzled with the sauce, topped with the cherry tomato halves and garnished with the parsley and mint. Accompany with the minted yoghurt.

Note Lebanese zucchini are plump and pale green.

CHICKPEA, CORN AND SEMI-DRIED TOMATO PATTIES WITH ROCKET SALAD

preparation time 20 minutes plus overnight soaking and 30 minutes chilling
cooking time 20 minutes
serves 4

225 g (8 oz/1 cup) dried chickpeas
1 small brown onion, coarsely
    chopped
2 garlic cloves
1 tablespoon sweet paprika
1 small red chilli, seeded and chopped
½ teaspoon salt
½ teaspoon freshly ground black
    pepper
1 egg, lightly whisked
1 handful basil leaves
1 large handful flat-leaf (Italian)
    parsley
100 g (3½ oz/½ cup) fresh corn
    kernels, or 100 g (3½ oz/⅔ cup)
    frozen corn kernels, thawed
30 g (1 oz/¼ cup) chopped
    semi-dried (sun-blushed) tomatoes
vegetable oil, for deep-frying

ROCKET SALAD
2 large handfuls rocket (arugula)
    leaves
200 g (7 oz) cherry tomatoes, halved
100 g (3½ oz/1 cup) shaved pecorino
    cheese
60 ml (2 fl oz/¼ cup) extra virgin olive
    oil
1 tablespoon lemon juice

- Place the chickpeas in a large bowl and cover with cold water. Leave to soak overnight.

- Drain the chickpeas and place in a food processor with the onion, garlic, paprika, chilli, salt and pepper. Blend until the chickpeas are the size of coarse breadcrumbs and the consistency is pasty. Add the egg, herbs, half the corn and half the tomato, and blend until the mixture just starts to come together. Transfer the mixture to a bowl. Add the remaining tomato and corn to the mixture. Mix together well, then cover and refrigerate for 30 minutes.

- Shape the mixture into 8 patties, about 7 cm (2¾ inches) in diameter.

- Preheat the oven to 150°C (300°F/Gas 2). Heat 1 cm (½ inch) oil in a large frying pan over medium heat. Working in batches, cook the patties for 2 minutes on each side, or until a deep golden brown. Drain on paper towels and keep warm in the oven while cooking the remaining patties.

- To make the rocket salad, put the rocket, tomatoes and pecorino in a serving bowl. Whisk together the olive oil and lemon juice, and season with sea salt and freshly ground black pepper. Pour the dressing over the salad and toss gently to coat.

- Pile the rocket salad on serving plates, top with the patties and serve.

GREEK RED LENTIL AND POTATO RISSOLES

preparation time 45 minutes plus 1 hour chilling
cooking time 50 minutes
serves 4

2 potatoes (about 380 g/13½ oz),
   peeled and chopped
400 g (14 oz/1⅔ cups) red lentils
2 tablespoons olive oil
1 small fennel bulb (about 250 g/
   9 oz), trimmed, tough core
   removed, then finely chopped
1 brown onion, finely chopped
2 garlic cloves, crushed
40 g (1½ oz/¼ cup) pitted kalamata
   olives, coarsely chopped
45 g (1½ oz/⅓ cup) chopped semi-
   dried (sun-blushed) tomatoes

75 g (2½ oz/½ cup) crumbled feta
   cheese
1 handful flat-leaf (Italian) parsley,
   chopped
1 handful mint leaves, chopped
2 eggs
1 tablespoon milk
75 g (2½ oz/½ cup) plain
   (all-purpose) flour
180 g (6 oz/2¼ cups) fresh
   breadcrumbs, lightly toasted
125 ml (4 fl oz/½ cup) vegetable oil
sea salt, to sprinkle
lemon wedges, to serve

• Place the potato in a small saucepan, cover with cold water and bring to the boil over medium–high heat. Cook for 15–20 minutes, or until the potato is tender. Drain, mash well and set aside.

• Meanwhile, rinse the lentils under cold running water, then drain. Place in a saucepan of lightly salted water and bring to the boil. Reduce the heat to low and simmer gently for 20–30 minutes, or until tender. Drain well and set aside.

• Heat the olive oil in a heavy-based frying pan over medium–low heat. Add the fennel, onion and garlic and cook, stirring, for 10–15 minutes, or until the fennel is tender. Transfer to a large bowl and allow to cool.

• Add the mashed potato and lentils to the fennel mixture, along with the olives, tomato, feta, parsley and mint. Season to taste with sea salt and freshly ground black pepper and mix until well combined. Form into 12 rissoles, using about ⅓ cup of mixture at a time, and place on a tray. Cover and refrigerate for 1 hour.

• In a small bowl, whisk together the eggs and milk. Place the flour and breadcrumbs in two separate shallow bowls. Coat the rissoles in the flour, next dip them in the egg wash, allowing the excess to run off, then finally coat them in the breadcrumbs.

• Heat half the oil in a large heavy-based frying pan over medium heat. Working in batches, and adding the remaining oil as needed, cook the rissoles for 2–3 minutes on each side, or until golden and warmed through.

• Drain on paper towels, then sprinkle with sea salt. Serve with lemon wedges.

PUMPKIN AND HAZELNUT PESTO BITES

preparation time 20 minutes
cooking time 35 minutes
makes 48

750 g (1 lb 10 oz) butternut pumpkin
   (squash)
30 ml (1 fl oz) oil
2 tablespoons freshly grated
   parmesan cheese (optional)

HAZELNUT PESTO
35 g (1 oz/¼ cup) roasted hazelnuts
35 g (1 oz) rocket (arugula)
1 tablespoon freshly grated parmesan
   cheese
30 ml (1 fl oz) oil

- Preheat the oven to 200°C (400°F/Gas 6). Peel the pumpkin and cut into
2 cm (¾ inch) slices, then cut into rough triangular shapes about 3 cm
(1¼ inches) along the base. Toss with the oil and some salt and black pepper
until coated. Spread on a baking tray and bake for 35 minutes, or until cooked.

- Meanwhile, to make the hazelnut pesto, process the hazelnuts, rocket,
parmesan and oil, until they form a paste, then season to taste.

- Spoon a small amount of the hazelnut pesto
onto each piece of baked pumpkin and
sprinkle with parmesan, if using, and
some black pepper. Serve warm or cold.

MUSHROOMS WITH HERB NUT BUTTER

preparation time 20 minutes
cooking time 20 minutes
serves 4–6

12 large mushrooms
1 tablespoon olive oil
1 small onion, finely chopped
40 g (1½ oz) blanched almonds
1 garlic clove, chopped
1 tablespoon lemon juice
3 tablespoons parsley sprigs

3 teaspoons chopped thyme or
 1 teaspoon dried thyme
3 teaspoons chopped rosemary or
 1 teaspoon dried rosemary
1 tablespoon snipped chives
75 g (3 oz) butter, chopped

● Preheat the oven to 180°C (350°F/Gas 4). Brush a shallow ovenproof dish
with a little oil or melted butter. Remove the stalks from the mushrooms and
finely chop the stalks. Heat the oil in a small frying pan, then add the onion.
Cook over medium heat for 2–3 minutes, or until soft and golden. Add the
chopped mushroom stalks. Cook for 2 minutes, or until softened. Remove from
the heat.

● Put the almonds, garlic, lemon juice, parsley, thyme, rosemary, chives, butter,
½ teaspoon salt and ¼ teaspoon pepper in a food processor. Process for
20–30 seconds, or until the mixture is smooth.

● Place the mushroom caps in the ovenproof dish. Spoon equal amounts of
the onion and mushroom mixture into each cap and smooth the surface. Top
each mushroom with the almond and herb mixture. Bake for 10–15 minutes,
or until the mushrooms are cooked through and the butter has melted.

note *Mushrooms are best cooked just before serving. Assemble the caps up to 2 hours before
serving and store, covered, on a flat tray, in the refrigerator.*

MUSHROOMS BAKED WITH TALEGGIO, HERBS AND GARLIC CRUMBS

preparation time 15 minutes
cooking time 30 minutes
serves 4

1 tablespoon olive oil
8 (about 850 g/1 lb 14 oz) medium-
 large flat mushrooms, peeled
60 g (2 oz) butter, melted
½ leek, white part only, washed and
 thinly sliced
2 garlic cloves, finely chopped
2 tablespoons white wine

100 g (3½ oz/1¼ cups) fresh
 breadcrumbs
1 teaspoon thyme leaves
1 tablespoon flat-leaf (Italian) parsley,
 finely chopped, plus whole leaves,
 to serve
200 g (7 oz) Taleggio cheese, cut into
 8 even slices

● Preheat the oven to 180°C (350°F/Gas 4). Brush a baking tray with the oil.
Remove the stems from the mushrooms. Finely chop the stems and set the
caps aside.

● Heat 40 g (1½ oz) of the butter in a small frying pan over low heat and add
the leek, garlic and mushroom stems. Cook, stirring often, for 5 minutes or until
softened, then add the wine and cook for 3 minutes. Remove from the heat
and place in a bowl, add the breadcrumbs, herbs and remaining butter. Season
to taste with sea salt and freshly ground black pepper and mix well.

● Place the mushroom caps on the prepared baking tray in a single layer, cap
side up. Fill each cap with a slice of Taleggio cheese, then divide the crumb
mixture evenly among the mushrooms. Bake for 20 minutes, or until the
mushrooms are tender and golden. Serve warm topped with parsley leaves.

BAKED RICOTTA

preparation time 15 minutes
cooking time 30 minutes
serves 8–12

2 kg (4 lb 8 oz) whole ricotta cheese
185 ml (6 fl oz/¾ cup) olive oil
185 ml (6 fl oz/¾ cup) lemon juice
2 tablespoons thin strips lemon zest
2 garlic cloves, crushed
25 g (1 oz) finely shredded basil
    leaves

50 g (2 oz/⅓ cup) semi-dried
    (sun-blushed) tomatoes, roughly
    chopped
Italian-style bread or bruschetta,
    to serve

• Remove any paper from the base of the ricotta and put the ricotta in a plastic colander. Place over a bowl, ensuring the base of the colander is not touching the base of the bowl. Cover with plastic wrap and leave overnight in the refrigerator, to drain.

• Preheat the oven to 250°C (500°F/Gas 9). Line a baking tray with baking paper. Transfer the ricotta to the tray and brush with a little of the olive oil. Bake for 30 minutes, or until golden brown. Allow to cool slightly.

• Mix the remaining olive oil, lemon juice and zest, garlic and basil in a bowl and season to taste. Place the whole ricotta on a platter, pour on the dressing and scatter with the semi-dried tomatoes. Serve with thin slices of Italian-style bread or bruschetta.

BROAD BEAN AND HALOUMI FRITTERS WITH WALNUT YOGHURT DIP

preparation time 20 minutes plus 2 hours standing
cooking time 45 minutes
serves 4

1 desiree potato (about 120 g/4 oz)
400 g (14 oz/2½ cups) frozen broad (fava) beans
1 egg, lightly beaten
1 small handful dill sprigs, plus extra, to garnish
1 small handful mint leaves, plus extra, to garnish
1 teaspoon finely grated lemon rind
1 tablespoon lemon juice
1 teaspoon ground cumin
¼ teaspoon chilli powder
150 g (5½ oz) haloumi cheese, coarsely grated

2 teaspoons plain (all-purpose) flour
vegetable oil for pan-frying

WALNUT YOGHURT DIP
2 slices day-old white bread, crusts removed
60 g (2 oz/½ cup) walnut pieces, lightly toasted
2 garlic cloves, crushed
1 teaspoon sea salt
2 teaspoons red wine vinegar, or to taste
2 tablespoons olive oil
250 g (9 oz/1 cup) Greek-style yoghurt

● To make the walnut yoghurt dip, place the bread, walnuts, garlic, salt, vinegar and olive oil in a food processor. Blend until a coarse paste forms, then transfer to a bowl and stir in the yoghurt. Stir in 1–2 tablespoons warm water to loosen the sauce. Cover and refrigerate for 2 hours.

● Cook the whole potato in a saucepan of boiling water for 20 minutes or until very tender when tested with a skewer. Drain. When cool enough to handle, peel away the skin, then mash the flesh with a fork until smooth. Set aside.

- Cook the broad beans in a saucepan of boiling water for 2 minutes, or until tender. Drain and leave until cool enough to handle, then peel.

- Place the broad beans in a food processor with the egg, dill, mint, lemon rind, lemon juice, cumin and chilli powder. Blend just until a coarse paste forms — do not overprocess as the mixture should still be a little chunky. Transfer to a bowl, then stir through the mashed potato, haloumi and flour.

- Pour enough oil into a large frying pan just to cover the base and place over medium heat. When the oil is hot, drop tablespoons of the mixture into it, flattening each one slightly. Cook the fritters in batches for 2 minutes on each side, or until deep golden and heated through — take care not to overcook them or the fritters will burn. Drain on paper towels while cooking the remaining fritters.

- Serve the fritters garnished with extra dill and mint, and accompanied by the walnut yoghurt dip.

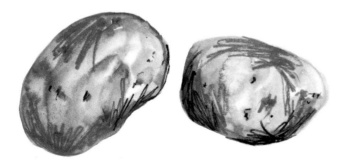

BUCKWHEAT BLINIS WITH MUSHROOMS

preparation time 20 minutes plus 1 hour 30 minutes proving
cooking time 25 minutes
serves 6

35 g (1 oz/¼ cup) plain (all-purpose)
   flour
35 g (1 oz/¼ cup) buckwheat flour
3 teaspoons caster (superfine) sugar
½ teaspoon active dry yeast
125 ml (4 fl oz/½ cup) milk
25 g (1 oz) butter, chopped, plus
   extra melted butter, for cooking
1 large egg, lightly beaten
2 spring onions (scallions), thinly
   sliced, to garnish

MUSHROOM TOPPING
20 g (¾ oz) butter
750 g (1 lb 10 oz) Swiss brown
   mushrooms, thinly sliced
2 garlic cloves, crushed
1½ tablespoons lemon juice
125 g (4½ oz/½ cup) crème fraîche
   or sour cream
1 tablespoon thyme leaves, finely
   chopped

● In a large bowl, combine the flours, sugar, yeast and ¼ teaspoon salt. Heat the milk and 25 g (1 oz) butter in a saucepan over low heat, stirring until the butter melts and the mixture is lukewarm. Add the milk mixture to the dry ingredients, whisking until smooth. Cover the batter with plastic wrap or a tea (dish) towel, leave in a draught-free, warm spot and allow to rise for 1–1½ hours or until doubled in size. Preheat the oven to 120°C (235°F/Gas ½).

● Meanwhile, for the mushroom topping, melt the butter in a large frying pan over medium heat. Add the mushroom to the pan and cook, stirring often, for 10 minutes or until the mushrooms are starting to brown and all the liquid has evaporated. Add the garlic and lemon juice and cook for 1 minute. Remove the pan from the heat and stir in the crème fraîche and thyme. Set aside while the blinis cook.

• Deflate the blini batter with a whisk and whisk in the egg.

• Heat a large frying pan over medium heat and brush lightly with melted butter. Working in batches, add 60 ml (2 fl oz/¼ cup) cupfuls of batter to the pan and cook for 2–3 minutes or until bubbles appear on the surface. Turn the blinis and cook for 1 minute or until golden brown and cooked through. Transfer blinis as they cook to a warmed plate, cover loosely with foil and keep warm in the oven.

• To serve, divide blinis among plates, top each with some of the mushroom mixture and decorate with spring onion curls.

BROAD BEAN, VEGETABLE AND RICOTTA PASTA ROLLS

preparation time 30 minutes
cooking time 55 minutes
serves 4

750 g (1 lb 10 oz) orange sweet
   potato, peeled and chopped
1 tablespoon olive oil
½ teaspoon chilli flakes
235 g (8½ oz/1½ cups) frozen peas
115 g (4 oz/¾ cup) frozen broad (fava)
   beans
375 g (13 oz/1½ cups) fresh ricotta
   cheese
35 g (1 oz/⅓ cup) grated parmesan
   cheese
1½ teaspoons finely grated lemon
   rind
4 fresh lasagne sheets (each about
   10 x 14 cm/4 x 5½ inches)
40 g (1½ oz) butter
2 teaspoons lemon juice
1 tablespoon small basil leaves

**BABY ENGLISH SPINACH AND
   WALNUT SALAD**
90 g (3 oz/2 cups) baby English
   spinach leaves
40 g (1½ oz/⅓ cup) chopped toasted
   hazelnuts
2 tablespoons extra virgin olive oil
1½ tablespoons lemon juice

- Preheat the oven to 180°C (350°F/Gas 4). Place the sweet potato in a baking dish. Drizzle with the olive oil, sprinkle with the chilli flakes and season to taste with sea salt and freshly ground black pepper. Toss to combine, then bake for 25 minutes, or until tender. Remove from the oven and leave to cool.

- Meanwhile, cook the peas and broad beans in a small saucepan of boiling water for 3 minutes, or until tender. Drain. When the broad beans are cool enough to handle, peel and discard the skins. Leave to cool.

- Combine the sweet potato, peas and broad beans in a bowl, then roughly crush using a fork. Add the ricotta, parmesan and lemon rind and mix well.

- Place a lasagne sheet on a cutting board. Spoon about ¼ cup of the pea mixture evenly over the pasta, then roll up like a Swiss roll. Brush the edges with water, and press together to seal. Repeat with the remaining pasta and filling. Wrap each roll tightly in plastic wrap, then foil.

- Gently lower the rolls into a large saucepan of simmering water. Place a plate on top to keep them submerged. Cook for 25 minutes, then remove the rolls from the water with a slotted spoon and leave to stand for 5 minutes.

- While the rolls are standing, make the baby English spinach and walnut salad. Combine the spinach and hazelnuts in a bowl, drizzle with the olive oil and toss gently to combine. Sprinkle with the lemon juice and season to taste.

- Just before serving, melt the butter in a frying pan over high heat for 2 minutes, or until lightly browned. Add the lemon juice and basil and stir to combine. Season to taste.

- Slice each roll into three pieces and place on serving plates. Drizzle with the burnt butter sauce and serve with the salad.

HERBED CHEESE CRACKERS

preparation time 40 minutes
cooking time 16 minutes
serves 4–6

PASTRY
125 g (4½ oz/1 cup) plain
   (all-purpose) flour
½ teaspoon baking powder
60 g (2 oz) butter
1 egg, lightly beaten
60 g (2 oz) cheddar cheese, grated
1 teaspoon snipped chives
1 teaspoon chopped flat-leaf (Italian)
   parsley (see Notes)
1 tablespoon iced water

CHEESE FILLING
80 g (3 oz) cream cheese, softened
20 g (¾ oz) butter
1 tablespoon snipped chives
1 tablespoon chopped flat-leaf
   (Italian) parsley (see Notes)
¼ teaspoon lemon pepper
90 g (3 oz) cheddar cheese, grated

● Preheat the oven to 190°C (375°F/Gas 5). Line two baking trays with baking paper. To make the pastry, sift the flour and baking powder into a large bowl and add the chopped butter. Rub in the butter with your fingertips, until the mixture resembles fine breadcrumbs.

● Make a well in the centre and add the egg, cheese, herbs and iced water. Mix with a flat-bladed knife, using a cutting action, until the mixture comes together in beads. Gently gather together and lift out onto a lightly floured surface. Press together into a ball.

- Roll the pastry between sheets of baking paper to 3 mm (⅛ inch) thick. Remove the top sheet of paper and cut the pastry into rounds, using a 5 cm (2 inch) cutter. Place the rounds onto the baking trays. Re-roll the remaining pastry and repeat the cutting process. Bake for about 8 minutes, or until lightly browned. Transfer to a wire rack to cool.

- To make the filling, beat the cream cheese and butter in a small bowl using electric beaters until light and creamy. Add the herbs, pepper and cheese and beat until smooth. Spread ½ teaspoon of filling on half of the biscuits and sandwich together with the remaining biscuits.

Notes *You can use chopped lemon thyme instead of parsley. The biscuits can be made 2 days ahead and stored in an airtight container, or frozen.*
The filling can be made a day ahead and stored, covered, in the refrigerator.

PARMESAN AND PESTO TOASTS

preparation time 30 minutes
cooking time 5 minutes
serves 8–10

1 baguette
16 large sun-dried tomatoes
150 g (5½ oz) parmesan cheese,
   thinly shaved

PESTO
50 g (2 oz) basil leaves
2 tablespoons snipped chives
50 g (2 oz/⅓ cup) pine nuts
2–3 garlic cloves
60 ml (2 fl oz/¼ cup) olive oil

● Freeze the baguette until firm. Cut it into very thin slices, using a sharp serrated knife. Toast the slices under a hot grill (broiler) until they are golden brown on both sides. Cut the sun-dried tomatoes into thin strips.

● To make the pesto, put all of the ingredients in a food processor. Process for 20–30 seconds, or until smooth.

● Spread the pesto mixture evenly over the toasted baguette slices. Top with strips of sun-dried tomato and shavings of parmesan cheese.

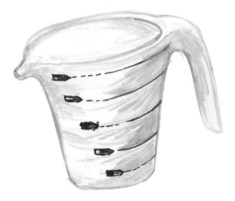

CHEESE AND CHIVE SCONES

preparation time 20 minutes
cooking time 12 minutes
makes 9

250 g (9 oz/2 cups) self-raising flour
30 g (1 oz) butter, chopped
60 g (2 oz/½ cup) grated cheddar
   cheese
3 tablespoons shredded parmesan
   cheese

2 tablespoons snipped chives
125 ml (4 fl oz/½ cup) milk
3 tablespoons grated cheddar cheese,
   extra

• Preheat the oven to 210°C (415°F/Gas 6–7). Brush a baking tray with melted butter or oil. Sift the flour and a pinch of salt into a bowl. Rub in the butter using your fingertips. Stir in the cheeses and the chives. Make a well in the centre, add the milk and almost all of 125 ml (4 fl oz/½ cup) water. Mix lightly with a flat-bladed knife to form a soft dough, adding more water if the dough is too dry.

• Knead the dough briefly on a lightly floured surface until smooth. Press out the dough to 2 cm (¾ inch) thick. Using a floured 5 cm (2 inch) plain round cutter, cut nine rounds from the dough. Place the rounds on the prepared tray and sprinkle with the extra cheese. Bake for 12 minutes, or until the cheese is golden brown.

Snacks & small bites

POTATO AND OLIVE SCONES

preparation time 25 minutes
cooking time 15 minutes
makes 15

250 g (9 oz) potatoes, chopped
125 ml (4 fl oz/½ cup) milk
250 g (9 oz/2 cups) self-raising flour
30 g (1 oz) butter, chopped

3 tablespoons black olives, pitted and chopped
3–4 teaspoons chopped rosemary
milk, extra, to glaze

● Preheat the oven to 210°C (415°F/Gas 6–7). Brush a baking tray with melted butter or oil. Boil or microwave the potatoes until tender. Mash the potatoes with the milk and season with freshly ground black pepper.

● Sift the flour into a large bowl. Rub in the butter, using your fingertips. Add the olives and rosemary and stir until just combined. Make a well in the centre and add the mashed potato and almost all of 125 ml (4 fl oz/½ cup) water. Mix with a flat-bladed knife, using a cutting action, until the mixture forms a soft dough. Add more water if the dough is too dry.

● Knead the dough briefly on a lightly floured surface until smooth. Press out to a thickness of 2 cm (¾ inch). Using a floured 5 cm (2 inch) plain round cutter, cut 15 rounds from the dough and place them on the prepared tray. Brush the tops with the extra milk and cook for about 10–15 minutes until the scones are golden brown.

MINI ONION AND PARMESAN SCONES

preparation time 25 minutes
cooking time 12 minutes
makes 24

30 g (1 oz) butter
1 small onion, finely chopped
250 g (9 oz/2 cups) self-raising flour,
   sifted

50 g (2 oz/½ cup) finely shredded
   fresh parmesan cheese
125 ml (4 oz/½ cup) milk
cayenne pepper, to sprinkle

● Preheat the oven to 210°C (415°F/Gas 6–7). Brush a baking tray with a little melted butter or oil.

● Melt the butter in a small frying pan, add the onion and cook, over low heat, for 2–3 minutes or until soft. Cool slightly.

● Combine the sifted flour, parmesan and a pinch salt in a bowl. Make a well in the centre and add the onion. Combine the milk with 125 ml (4 oz/½ cup) water and add almost all to the bowl. Mix lightly, with a flat-bladed knife, using a cutting action, until the mixture forms a soft dough. Add more liquid if the dough is too dry. Knead dough briefly on a lightly floured surface until smooth and press out to 2 cm (¾ inch) thick. Cut the dough into 24 rounds with a 3 cm (1¼ inch) plain round cutter. Place the rounds on the prepared tray and sprinkle each with a little cayenne pepper. Cook for 10–12 minutes until the scones are golden brown.

Snacks & small bites

Note: Handle scone dough with a light touch. Cut the liquid in with a knife and then take care not to over-knead or you'll have tough scones.

CAPSICUM AND CORN MUFFINS

preparation time 15 minutes
cooking time 20 minutes
makes 12

125 g (4½ oz/1 cup) plain
  (all-purpose) flour
1 tablespoon baking powder
150 g (5½ oz/1 cup) fine polenta
1 tablespoon caster (superfine) sugar
1 egg
170 ml (5½ fl oz/⅔ cup) milk
¼ teaspoon Tabasco sauce (optional)

60 ml (2 fl oz/¼ cup) oil
½ red capsicum (pepper), seeded,
  membrane removed and finely
  chopped
440 g (15½ oz) tinned corn kernels,
  drained
3 tablespoons finely chopped flat-leaf
  (Italian) parsley

● Preheat the oven to 210°C (415°F/Gas 6–7). Brush a 12-hole muffin tin with oil or melted butter. Sift the flour, baking powder and ¼ teaspoon salt into a large bowl. Add the polenta and sugar. Stir thoroughly until all the ingredients are well mixed. Make a well in the centre.

● Combine the egg, milk, Tabasco and oil in a separate bowl. Add the egg mixture, capsicum, corn and parsley all at once to the dry ingredients. Stir quickly with a wooden spoon or rubber spatula until all the ingredients are just moistened. (Do not over-mix — the batter should be quite lumpy.)

● Spoon the mixture into the tin. Bake for 20 minutes, or until golden. Loosen with a knife but leave in the tin for 2 minutes. Cool on a wire rack.

ZUCCHINI AND CARROT MUFFINS

preparation time 20 minutes
cooking time 20 minutes
makes 12

2 zucchini (courgettes)
2 carrots
250 g (9 oz/2 cups) self-raising flour
1 teaspoon ground cinnamon
½ teaspoon freshly grated nutmeg

60 g (2 oz/½ cup) chopped pecans
2 eggs
250 ml (9 fl oz/1 cup) milk
90 g (3 oz) butter, melted

● Preheat the oven to 210°C (415°F/Gas 6–7). Brush a 12-hole muffin tin with melted butter or oil. Grate the zucchini and carrots. Sift the flour, cinnamon, nutmeg and a pinch of salt into a large bowl. Add the carrot, zucchini and chopped pecans. Stir thoroughly until all the ingredients are well combined.

● Combine the eggs, milk and melted butter in a separate bowl and whisk well until combined.

● Make a well in the centre of the flour mixture and add the egg mixture all at once. Mix quickly with a fork or rubber spatula until all the ingredients are just moistened. (Do not over-mix — the batter should be quite lumpy.)

● Spoon the batter evenly into the prepared tin. Bake for 15–20 minutes, or until golden. Loosen the muffins with a flat-bladed knife or spatula and leave in the tin for 2 minutes, before turning out onto a wire rack to cool.

Snacks & small bites

55

Soups & salads

These sustaining soups and salads include flavoursome ingredients beloved of many different cuisines.

CHILLED CUCUMBER SOUP WITH CURRY OIL

preparation time 20 minutes plus 2 hours chillihg
cooking time 2 minutes
serves 4–6

3 telegraph (long) cucumbers, peeled, seeded and coarsely chopped
3 spring onions (scallions), trimmed and thinly sliced
1 garlic clove
125 g (4½ oz/½ cup) plain Greek-style yoghurt
2 tablespoons lime juice

2 tablespoons sour cream
Tabasco sauce, to taste (optional)
185 ml (6 fl oz/¾ cup) vegetable stock
1 small handful mint, chopped
290 ml (10 fl oz) vegetable oil
½ teaspoon curry powder
4 x 15 cm (6 inch) poppadoms

● Combine the cucumber, onion, garlic, yoghurt, lime juice, sour cream, Tabasco, if using, stock and mint in a food processor and process until a smooth purée forms. Season to taste with sea salt and freshly ground black pepper, then transfer to a bowl, cover and refrigerate for 2 hours or until well chilled.

● Heat 2 tablespoons of the oil in a small saucepan, add the curry powder and cook over medium heat for 30 seconds, or until fragrant, then cool.

● Heat the remaining oil in a small frying pan until almost smoking. Add the poppadoms, in batches, and cook for 4–5 seconds or until puffed and golden. Remove with a slotted spoon and drain on paper towels. When cool enough to handle, roughly break into small pieces.

● Serve the soup in bowls, drizzled with the curry oil and topped with poppadom pieces.

GREEN GAZPACHO WITH ROAST ALMONDS

preparation time 20 minutes plus 2 hours chilling
cooking time Nil
serves 6

2–4 garlic cloves, chopped

3 spring onions (scallions), trimmed and chopped

2 Lebanese (short) cucumbers (about 350 g/12 oz), peeled and chopped

1 green capsicum (pepper) (about 250 g/9 oz), seeded and chopped

80 g (3 oz) day-old bread, chopped

½ an iceberg lettuce, outer leaves discarded, chopped

2 large handfuls flat-leaf (Italian) parsley, chopped

1 large handful coriander (cilantro) leaves, chopped

310–375 ml (10¾–13 fl oz/ 1¼–1½ cups) vegetable stock

250 ml (9 fl oz/1 cup) extra virgin olive oil

60 ml (2 fl oz/¼ cup) sherry vinegar, or to taste

80 g (3 oz/1½ cup) roasted almonds, coarsely chopped

● Combine the garlic, spring onion, cucumber, capsicum, bread, lettuce and herbs in a large bowl. Working in batches, process the mixture in a food processor, adding a little of the stock to each batch, until a purée forms.

● Transfer the purée to a large bowl, then stir in 185 ml (6 fl oz/¾ cup) of the olive oil and the sherry vinegar. Season to taste with sea salt and freshly ground black pepper.

● Cover the bowl tightly, then refrigerate for 2 hours or until well chilled.

● Divide the soup among bowls and serve sprinkled with chopped almonds and drizzled with remaining olive oil.

Soups & salads

LEMONGRASS, CORN AND COCONUT SOUP

preparation time 45 minutes
cooking time 55 minutes
serves 4–6

1½ tablespoons coarsely chopped
    fresh ginger
2 garlic cloves, chopped
2 lemongrass stems, white part only,
    thinly sliced
½ teaspoon ground turmeric
½ teaspoon chilli flakes, or to taste
60 ml (2 fl oz/¼ cup) peanut oil
1 large brown onion, finely chopped
4 corn cobs, kernels removed
2 desiree or other all-purpose
    potatoes (about 325 g/11½ oz),
    peeled and cut into 5 mm (¼ inch)
    cubes

1.25 litres (44 fl oz/5 cups) vegetable
    stock
2½ tablespoons soy sauce
400 ml (14 fl oz) tin coconut cream
2 spring onions (scallions), thinly
    sliced
ground white pepper, to taste
1 small handful chopped coriander
    (cilantro) leaves
2 kaffir lime leaves, very thinly sliced
1 small red chilli, or to taste, thinly
    sliced
80 g (3 oz/½ cup) roasted peanuts,
    coarsely chopped

● In a small food processor, combine the ginger, garlic, lemongrass, turmeric and chilli flakes and 1 tablespoon of the oil. Blend until a coarse paste forms.

● Heat the remaining oil in a large saucepan over medium–low heat. Add the onion and corn and cook, stirring often, for 10 minutes, or until the corn is starting to soften.

● Add the ginger mixture and potato, and stir until well combined. Cook over low heat for 2 minutes, or until aromatic.

● Stir in the stock, soy sauce and coconut cream and slowly bring to a simmer. Simmer gently for 35–40 minutes, or until the corn and potato are very tender.

● Transfer 750 ml (26 fl oz/3 cups) of the soup to a food processor and blend to a smooth purée. Return the puréed soup to the pan and reheat gently. Stir in the spring onion and season to taste with sea salt and ground white pepper.

● Ladle the soup into serving bowls. Serve garnished with the coriander, lime leaves, chilli and peanuts.

SWEET POTATO AND TOFU LAKSA

preparation time 30 minutes
cooking time 20 minutes
serves 1

50 g (2 oz/⅓ cup) chopped
   sweet potato
75 g (2½ oz/¾ cup) fresh thin
   rice noodles
2 teaspoons peanut oil
55 g (2 oz) ready-made laksa paste
250 ml (9 fl oz/1 cup) coconut milk
250 ml (9 fl oz/1 cup) vegetable stock
   or water
2 kaffir lime leaves, shredded
   (optional)
½ lemongrass stem, trimmed and
   sliced in half lengthways (optional)

5 cherry tomatoes, halved
75 g (3 oz) firm tofu, cut into
   2 cm (¾ inch) cubes
2 teaspoons soy sauce
1 teaspoon sweet chilli sauce
1 teaspoon lime juice
50 g (2 oz) trimmed snow peas
   (mangetout), halved diagonally
1 small handful coriander (cilantro)
   leaves
½ medium red chilli, sliced in half,
   seeded and thinly sliced (optional)

● Place the sweet potato in a steamer and cook for 7–10 minutes or until the flesh is just tender.

● Meanwhile, place the noodles in a heatproof bowl. Pour over boiling water, cover and stand for 5–10 minutes or until tender. Drain and place into a deep serving bowl.

● Heat the oil in a wok over high heat. Add the paste and cook, stirring, for 30 seconds or until fragrant.

● Pour in the coconut milk, stock or water and add the lime leaves and lemongrass, if using. Bring to the boil, reduce the heat to medium and cook gently for 3 minutes. Add the tomatoes and cook for 2–3 minutes or until just collapsing. Stir in the tofu, soy sauce, sweet chilli sauce, lime juice and snow peas. Cook for 1–2 minutes or until the tofu has warmed through and the snow peas are tender. Remove the lime leaves and lemongrass, if using.

● Spoon the laksa over the noodles and top with the coriander leaves and sliced chilli, if using. Serve immediately.

CREAMY CORN AND TOMATO SOUP

preparation time 20 minutes
cooking time 15 minutes
serves 4–6

1 teaspoon olive oil
1 teaspoon vegetable stock (bouillon)
   powder
1 onion, finely chopped
3 tomatoes
425 g (15 oz) tomato paste
   (concentrated purée)

310 g (11 oz) tinned creamed corn
125 g (4½ oz) tinned corn kernels,
   drained
chilli powder, to taste
sour cream and tortillas, to serve

● Heat the oil in a large saucepan. Add the stock powder and onion and cook until the onion is soft.

● Score a cross in the base of the tomatoes. Put in a heatproof bowl and cover with boiling water. Leave for 30 seconds, then transfer to cold water and peel the skin away from the cross. Cut the tomato in half, scoop out the seeds and chop the flesh.

● Add the tomato to the pan with the tomato paste, creamed corn and corn kernels. Season with chilli. Stir until heated through. Serve with a dollop of sour cream and some warm tortillas.

RED CAPSICUM SOUP

preparation time 20 minutes
cooking time 30 minutes
serves 6

4 red capsicums (peppers)
4 tomatoes
60 ml (2 fl oz/¼ cup) oil
½ teaspoon dried marjoram
½ teaspoon dried mixed herbs
2 garlic cloves, crushed

1 teaspoon mild curry paste
1 red onion, sliced
1 leek, white part only, sliced
250 g (9 oz) green cabbage, chopped
1 teaspoon sweet chilli sauce

• Cut the capsicums into quarters. Remove the seeds and membrane. Grill
(broil) until the skin blackens and blisters. Place on a cutting board, cover with a
tea towel (dish towel) and allow to cool before peeling and chopping.

• Score a cross in the base of the tomatoes. Put in a heatproof bowl and cover
with boiling water. Leave for 30 seconds, then transfer to cold water and peel
the skin away from the cross. Cut the tomatoes in half, scoop out the seeds and
chop the flesh.

• Heat the oil in a large saucepan. Add the herbs, garlic and curry paste. Stir
over low heat for 1 minute, or until aromatic. Add the onion and leek and cook
for 3 minutes or until golden. Add the cabbage, capsicum, tomato and 1 litre
(35 fl oz/4 cups) water. Bring to the boil, reduce heat and simmer for
20 minutes. Remove from the heat.

• Allow to cool slightly before transferring to a food processor and blending, in
batches, for 30 seconds, or until smooth. Return the soup to a clean saucepan,
stir through the chilli sauce and season to taste with salt and freshly ground
black pepper. Reheat gently and serve hot.

Soups & salads

QUINOA AND VEGETABLE SOUP

preparation time 20 minutes
cooking time 45 minutes
serves 4

2 tablespoons olive oil
1 large brown onion, finely chopped
2 carrots, finely chopped
2 celery stalks, finely chopped
2 garlic cloves, crushed
2 thyme sprigs
1 tablespoon ground fennel seeds
2 teaspoons ground cumin
1 teaspoon ground turmeric
750 ml (26 fl oz/3 cups) vegetable
  stock

500 g (1 lb 2 oz/2½ cups) chopped
  vine-ripened tomatoes
100 g (3½ oz/½ cup) quinoa
400 g (14 oz) tin chickpeas, rinsed
  and drained
3 tablespoons finely chopped flat-leaf
  (Italian) parsley leaves
60 g (2 oz/¼ cup) Greek-style
  yoghurt
lemon or lime wedges, to serve
  (optional)

● Heat the olive oil in a saucepan over medium–high heat. Add the onion, carrot and celery. Cook, stirring, for 10 minutes, or until the vegetables start to soften. Add the garlic, thyme sprigs, ground fennel, cumin and turmeric. Cook, stirring, for 1 minute, or until aromatic.

● Add the stock, tomatoes and 500 ml (17 fl oz/2 cups) water. Bring to the boil, then reduce the heat to low and simmer, uncovered, for 30 minutes.

● Meanwhile, cook the quinoa in a small saucepan of boiling water for 10 minutes, or until tender. Drain.

● Stir the quinoa, chickpeas and parsley into the soup and heat through.

● Ladle the soup into serving bowls. Serve with a dollop of yoghurt, and lemon or lime wedges if desired.

PAPPA AL POMODORO

preparation time 25 minutes
cooking time 25
serves 4

750 g (1 lb 10 oz) vine-ripened
   tomatoes
1 loaf (about 450 g/1 lb) day-old
   crusty Italian bread
1 tablespoon olive oil
3 garlic cloves, crushed

1 tablespoon tomato paste
   (concentrated purée)
1.25 litres (44 fl oz/5 cups) hot
   vegetable stock or water
1 tablespoon torn basil leaves
2–3 tablespoons extra virgin olive oil,
   plus extra, to serve

- Score a cross in the base of the tomatoes. Put in a heatproof bowl and cover with boiling water. Leave for 30 seconds, then transfer to cold water and peel the skin away from the cross. Cut the tomatoes in half, scoop out the seeds and chop the flesh.

- Discard most of the crust from the bread and tear the bread into 3 cm (1¼ inch) pieces.

- Heat the oil in a large saucepan. Add the garlic, tomato and tomato paste, then reduce the heat and simmer, stirring occasionally, for 10–15 minutes, or until reduced. Add the stock and bring to the boil, stirring for about 3 minutes. Reduce the heat to medium, add the bread pieces and cook, stirring, for 5 minutes, or until the bread softens and absorbs most of the liquid. Add more stock or water if the soup is too thick. Remove from the heat.

- Stir in the basil and extra virgin olive oil, and leave for 5 minutes so the flavours have time to develop. Serve drizzled with a little extra virgin olive oil.

ROAST TOMATO, SWEET POTATO AND ORANGE SOUP

preparation time 35 minutes
cooking time 1 hour 15 minutes
serves 6

1.5 kg (3 lb 5 oz) sweet potato, peeled and cut into 3 cm (1¼ inch) chunks

2 tablespoons thyme leaves, plus extra, to garnish

100 ml (3½ fl oz) olive oil

4 vine-ripened tomatoes (about 550 g/1 lb 4 oz), chopped

3 garlic cloves, chopped

1 tablespoon chopped sage, plus extra sage leaves, to garnish

2 teaspoons balsamic vinegar

2 brown onions, thinly sliced

2 carrots, cut into 1 cm (½ inch) chunks

2 celery stalks, thinly sliced

2.5 litres (87 fl oz/10 cups) vegetable stock

60 ml (2 fl oz/¼ cup) freshly squeezed orange juice

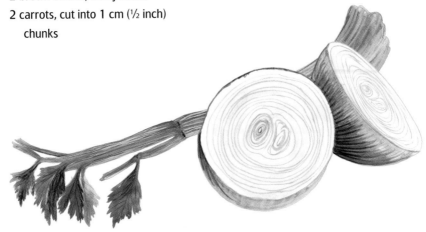

- Preheat the oven to 180°C (350°F/Gas 4). Line two baking trays with baking paper. Place the sweet potato on one baking tray. Sprinkle with half the thyme and drizzle with 2 tablespoons of the olive oil. Season to taste with sea salt and freshly ground black pepper and toss to coat.

- Place the tomato, garlic and sage on the other baking tray. Drizzle with the vinegar and 1 tablespoon of the olive oil. Season to taste and toss to coat.

- Roast the sweet potato and tomato, swapping the trays halfway through cooking, for 35 minutes, or until the sweet potato is tender and golden and the tomato is just collapsing. Remove from the oven and set aside.

- Heat the remaining oil in a large saucepan over medium—low heat. Add the onion, carrot, celery and remaining thyme. Cook, stirring, for 10–15 minutes, or until the vegetables start to soften. Pour in the stock and orange juice, then add the roasted sweet potato, tomato and any cooking juices. Simmer, uncovered, for 25 minutes, or until the vegetables are tender. Remove from the heat and allow to cool slightly.

- Transfer the soup in batches to a food processor and process until smooth. Return the soup to the saucepan and bring to a simmer. Season to taste. Garnish with extra thyme and sage.

CREAM OF PARSNIP SOUP

preparation time 20 minutes
cooking time 4 hours 20 minutes
serves 4

1 kg (2 lb 4 oz) parsnips, peeled and chopped
200 g (7 oz) all-purpose potatoes, such as sebago, peeled and chopped
1 granny smith apple, peeled, cored and chopped

1 onion, finely chopped
1 garlic clove, chopped
750 ml (26 fl oz/3 cups) good-quality vegetable stock
a pinch of saffron threads
250 ml (9 fl oz/1 cup) cream
snipped chives, to serve

• Place the parsnip, potato, apple, onion, garlic, stock and saffron threads in a slow cooker. Cover and cook on high for 4 hours.

• Transfer the mixture to a food processor or blender, in batches if necessary. Purée to a soup consistency, then season to taste with sea salt.

• Return the soup to the slow cooker and stir in the cream. Cover and cook for a further 20 minutes.

• Ladle the soup into serving bowls. Serve sprinkled with chives and plenty of freshly ground black pepper.

Note This soup can also be cooked on the stove. You will need to add extra stock..

GREEN PEA SOUP

preparation time 20 minutes
cooking time 1 hour 40 minutes
serves 4–6

335 g (12 oz/1½ cups) dried green
   split peas
2 tablespoons oil
1 onion, finely chopped
1 celery stalk, finely sliced
1 carrot, finely sliced
1 tablespoon ground cumin
1 tablespoon ground coriander

2 teaspoons grated fresh ginger
1.25 litres (44 fl oz/5 cups) vegetable
   stock
310 g (11 oz/2 cups) frozen green
   peas
1 tablespoon chopped mint
yoghurt or sour cream, to serve

• Soak the split peas in cold water for 2 hours. Drain the peas well.

• Heat the oil in a large heavy-based saucepan and add the onion, celery and carrot. Cook over medium heat for 3 minutes, stirring occasionally, until soft but not browned. Stir in the cumin, coriander and ginger, then cook for 1 minute. Add the split peas and stock to pan. Bring to the boil, then reduce the heat to low. Simmer, covered, for 1½ hours, stirring occasionally. Add the frozen peas to the pan and stir to combine.

• Allow to cool slightly before transferring to a food processor and blending, in batches, until smooth. Return to a clean pan and gently reheat. Season to taste and then stir in the mint. Serve in bowls with a swirl of yoghurt or sour cream.

Soups & salads

CARROT SOUP WITH CORIANDER PESTO

preparation time 20 minutes
cooking time about 8 hours
serves 4

2 tablespoons olive oil
1 red onion, diced
1 garlic clove, finely chopped
1 teaspoon cumin seeds
1 teaspoon paprika
1 teaspoon garam masala
3 small red chillies, seeded and
finely chopped
6 large carrots, peeled and chopped
1 kg (2 lb 4 oz) sweet potatoes,
    peeled and diced
2 large desiree potatoes, peeled
and diced

1.5 litres (52 fl oz/6 cups) vegetable
    stock
300 ml (10½ fl oz) coconut cream
toasted naan bread, to serve

CORIANDER PESTO

45 g (1½ oz/¼ cup) cashew nuts
1 large handful coriander (cilantro)
leaves
1 small garlic clove, halved
60 ml (2 fl oz/¼ cup) coconut milk
60 ml (2 fl oz/¼ cup) olive oil

● Heat the olive oil in a frying pan over medium–high heat. Add the onion and garlic and cook, stirring often, for 2–3 minutes, or until the onion has softened. Stir in the spices and chilli and cook for a further 1 minute, or until aromatic.

● Spoon the onion and garlic mixture into a slow cooker and add the chopped vegetables and stock. Mix together well.

● Cover and cook on low for 8 hours.

● Meanwhile, near serving time, make the coriander pesto. Place the cashews, coriander, garlic and coconut milk in a food processor and process until the nuts are finely chopped. With the motor running, gradually add the olive oil in a thin steady stream until well combined.

• Using a stick blender, purée the soup until smooth. Stir the coconut cream through, then season to taste with sea salt and freshly ground black pepper.

• Ladle the soup into serving bowls. Swirl some of the pesto over the top and serve with toasted naan bread.

Note *This soup can also be cooked on the stove. You will need to add extra stock..*

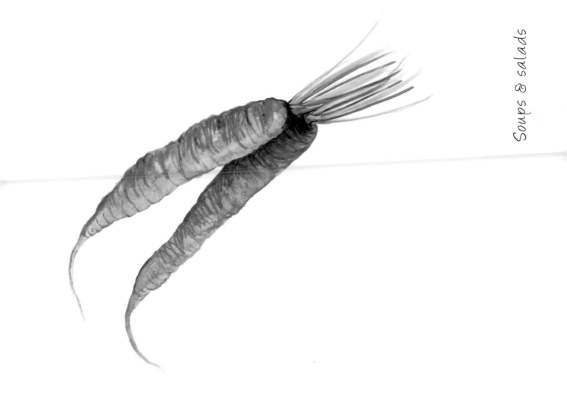

HEARTY VEGETABLE SOUP WITH GORGONZOLA TOASTS

preparation time 20 minutes
cooking time 1 hour 5 minutes
serves 4

2 tablespoons vegetable oil

1 onion, cut into 2 cm (¾ inch) chunks

1 leek, white part only, cut into 2 cm (¾ inch) chunks

1 carrot, thickly sliced

1 fresh bay leaf

1.25 litres (44 fl oz/5 cups) vegetable stock

400 g (14 oz) tin chopped tomatoes

2 tablespoons tomato paste (concentrated purée)

110 g (4 oz/½ cup) pearl barley

¼ white cabbage (about 300 g/10½ oz), core removed, then cut into 2 cm (¾ inch) chunks

400 g (14 oz) tin borlotti (cranberry) beans, rinsed and drained

1 small handful of chopped basil (optional)

GORGONZOLA TOASTS

4 slices of ciabatta or other rustic bread

100 g (3½ oz) Gorgonzola cheese, crumbled

● Heat the oil in a large heavy-based saucepan over medium heat. Add the onion, leek and carrot and sauté for 5 minutes, or until softened.

● Stir in the bay leaf, stock, tomatoes, tomato paste, barley and cabbage. Bring to the boil, then reduce the heat to medium−low. Cover and simmer for 1 hour, or until the vegetables and barley are tender. Season to taste with sea salt and freshly ground black pepper and stir in the borlotti beans. Bring back to a simmer, then reduce the heat to low, cover and keep warm.

• Meanwhile, make the Gorgonzola toasts. Heat the grill (broiler) to medium, then put the bread slices on a baking tray and cook under the grill for 2 minutes on each side, or until golden. Sprinkle the Gorgonzola over the toasts and grill (broil) until the cheese has melted.

• Ladle the soup into bowls and sprinkle with the basil, if using. Serve the soup with the hot Gorgonzola toasts.

.

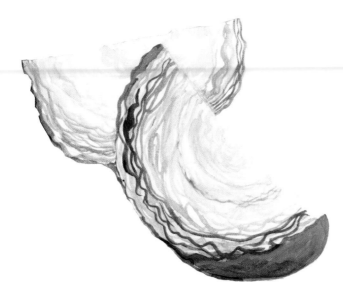

PUMPKIN, LENTIL AND TOMATO SOUP WITH CHEESY TOASTS

preparation time 20 minutes
cooking time 30 minutes
serves 4

2 tablespoons olive oil
1 kg (2 lb 4 oz) pumpkin (winter squash), peeled, seeded and cut into 2 cm (¾ inch) chunks
2 carrots, finely chopped
2 onions, finely chopped
1 large celery stalk, finely chopped
3 garlic cloves, crushed
1.5 litres (52 fl oz/6 cups) vegetable stock
125 g (4½ oz/½ cup) red lentils
400 g (14 oz) tin chopped tomatoes
1 tablespoon finely chopped parsley or coriander (cilantro) leaves

CHEESY TOASTS
8 slices of ciabatta or other rustic bread, cut about 2 cm (¾ inch) thick
85 g (3 oz/⅔ cup) finely grated cheddar cheese

- Heat the oil in a large saucepan over medium heat. Add the vegetables and garlic and sauté for 5 minutes, or until softened but not browned.

- Stir in the stock, lentils and tomatoes. Bring to the boil, then reduce the heat to medium–low and simmer for 20 minutes, or until the lentils are tender. Season well with sea salt and freshly ground black pepper.

- Meanwhile, make the cheesy toasts. Heat the grill (broiler) to medium, then place the bread slices on a baking tray and toast under the grill on one side. Turn the toasts over and scatter with the grated cheese. Grill for 3–4 minutes, or until the cheese has melted and is golden brown. Ladle the soup into bowls or cups, sprinkle with parsley and serve with the hot cheesy toasts.

LENTIL AND SILVERBEET SOUP

preparation time 20 minutes
cooking time 1 hour 30 minutes
serves 6

280 g (10 oz/1½ cups) brown lentils, washed
1 litre (35 fl oz/4 cups) vegetable stock
850 g (1 lb 14 oz) silverbeet (Swiss chard)
60 ml (2 fl oz/¼ cup) olive oil

1 large onion, finely chopped
4 garlic cloves, crushed
35 g (1 oz) finely chopped coriander (cilantro) leaves
80 ml (2½ fl oz/⅓ cup) lemon juice
lemon wedges, to serve

● Put the lentils in a large saucepan, then add the stock and 1 litre (35 fl oz/4 cups) water. Bring to the boil, then reduce the heat and simmer, covered, for 1 hour.

● Meanwhile, remove the stems from the silverbeet and shred the leaves. Heat the oil in a saucepan over medium heat and cook the onion for 2–3 minutes, or until transparent. Add the garlic and cook for 1 minute. Add the silverbeet and toss for 2–3 minutes, or until wilted. Stir the mixture into the lentils. Add the coriander and lemon juice, season, and simmer, covered, for 15–20 minutes. Serve with the lemon wedges.

CANNELLINI BEAN SOUP

preparation time 20 minutes plus overnight soaking
cooking time 1 hour 15 minutes
serves 8

500 g (1 lb 2 oz) dried cannellini
   beans
500 g (1 lb 2 oz) ripe tomatoes
2 tablespoons olive oil
2 onions, chopped
2 garlic cloves, crushed
3 tablespoons tomato passata
   (puréed tomatoes)

2 large carrots, diced
2 celery stalks, trimmed and diced
1.75 litres (59 fl oz/7 cups) vegetable
   stock
2 bay leaves
2 tablespoons lemon juice
30 g (1 oz) chopped flat-leaf (Italian)
   parsley

- Put the beans in a bowl, cover with cold water and leave the beans to soak overnight.

- Score a cross in the base of each tomato. Put in a heatproof bowl and cover with boiling water. Leave for 30 seconds then transfer to cold water and peel the skin away from the cross and roughly chop the flesh.

- Drain the beans and rinse under cold water. Heat the oil in a 5 litre (175 fl oz/20 cup) saucepan. Add the onion, reduce the heat and cook gently for 10 minutes, stirring occasionally. Stir in the garlic and cook for 1 minute. Add the cannellini beans, chopped tomato, passata, carrot, celery and stock. Add the bay leaves and stir. Bring to the boil, then reduce the heat to medium–low and simmer, covered, for 45–60 minutes, or until the beans are tender.

- Just before serving, stir in the lemon juice and season to taste. Stir in some of the parsley and use the rest as a garnish.

Soups & salads

FAST PASTA SOUP

preparation time 10 minutes
cooking time 10 minutes
serves 4

1 tablespoon oil
2 spring onions (scallions), chopped
150 g (5½ oz) snow peas
   (mangetout), trimmed and cut
   into pieces
200 g (7 oz) mushrooms, sliced

2 garlic cloves, crushed
1 teaspoon grated fresh ginger
1 litre (35 fl oz/4 cups) vegetable
   stock
150 g (5½ oz) angel hair pasta

• Heat the oil in a saucepan over medium heat and stir-fry the spring onion, snow peas and mushrooms for a few minutes, or until just tender.

• Add the garlic and grated fresh ginger and stir for 1 further minute. Pour in the vegetable stock and bring to the boil. Once boiling, add the pasta and cook for 3 minutes, or until just tender. Serve immediately.

RATATOUILLE AND PASTA SOUP

preparation time 25 minutes
cooking time 40 minutes
serves 6

1 eggplant (aubergine)
2 tablespoons olive oil
1 large onion, chopped
1 large red capsicum (pepper), chopped
1 large green capsicum (pepper), chopped
2 garlic cloves, crushed
3 zucchini (courgettes), sliced

800 g (1 lb 12 oz) tinned crushed tomatoes
1 teaspoon dried oregano leaves
½ teaspoon dried thyme leaves
1 litre (35 fl oz/4 cups) vegetable stock
50 g (2 oz) fusilli
fresh parmesan cheese shavings, to serve

● Chop the eggplant. To remove any bitterness, spread the eggplant pieces out in a colander and sprinkle generously with salt. Set aside for 20 minutes and then rinse thoroughly and pat dry with paper towels.

● Heat the oil in a large heavy-based saucepan and cook the onion over medium heat for 10 minutes, or until soft and lightly golden. Add the peppers, garlic, zucchini and eggplant and stir-fry for 5 minutes.

● Add the tomatoes, herbs and vegetable stock. Bring to the boil, reduce the heat and simmer for 10 minutes, or until the vegetables are tender. Add the fusilli and cook for a further 15 minutes, or until the fusilli is tender. Serve with shavings of parmesan scattered on top.

Soups & salads

CAPSICUM AND CHEESE BAKE WITH RADICCHIO AND OLIVE SALAD

preparation time 15 minutes
cooking time 1 hour 30 minutes
serves 4

1½ tablespoons olive oil, plus extra,
    for brushing
1 red capsicum (pepper), thinly sliced
75 g (2½ oz) butter
75 g (2½ oz/½ cup) plain
    (all-purpose) flour
750 ml (26 fl oz/3 cups) milk
75 g (2½ oz/¾ cup) grated pecorino
    cheese
2 eggs, plus 2 egg yolks
½ teaspoon freshly grated nutmeg, or
    to taste

RADICCHIO AND OLIVE SALAD
60 ml (2 fl oz/¼ cup) olive oil
2 heads of radicchio, trimmed,
    washed and patted dry, then cut
    into 8 wedges each
60 g (2 oz/½ cup) pitted black olives,
    sliced
1 small handful small basil leaves
1 tablespoon red wine vinegar

● Heat the oil in a frying pan over medium heat. Add the capsicum and cook, stirring, for 5–8 minutes, or until softened. Remove from the pan and set aside.

● Melt the butter in a saucepan over medium heat. Stir in the flour until smooth, then cook, stirring occasionally, for 2 minutes. Remove from the heat, then gradually add the milk, whisking constantly until combined. Return the pan to medium heat and stir until the mixture thickens and boils. Reduce the heat to low and simmer for 10 minutes, stirring to prevent lumps from forming. Remove from the heat, cover the surface of the sauce with a round of baking paper and set aside to cool for 5 minutes.

- Meanwhile, preheat the oven to 160°C (315°F/Gas 2–3). Brush four 185 ml (6 fl oz/¾ cup) ramekins with olive oil.

- In a large bowl, combine the cooled béchamel sauce with the pecorino, eggs, egg yolks and nutmeg, then season to taste with sea salt and freshly ground black pepper.

- Divide the capsicum slices among the ramekins. Top with the sauce mixture. Place the ramekins in a baking dish and pour enough boiling water into the baking dish to come three-quarters up the side of the ramekins. Transfer to the oven and bake for 60–70 minutes, or until the mixture has set. Remove the ramekins from the oven and leave to stand for 15 minutes.

- Meanwhile, make the radicchio and olive salad. Heat 2 tablespoons of the olive oil in a frying pan over medium–high heat. Add the radicchio and cook for 1–2 minutes, or until lightly browned. In a large bowl combine the remaining oil, olives, basil and vinegar. Add the warm radicchio and toss to combine. Arrange on a platter or on individual serving plates.

- Turn the capsicum bakes out of the ramekins and place on the salad, capsicum side up. Serve immediately.

ROAST PARSNIP, PUMPKIN, CHESTNUT AND PEAR SALAD

preparation time 15 minutes
cooking time 45 minutes
serves 4–6

3 parsnips (about 450 g/1 lb)
2 beurre bosc pears
8 thyme sprigs
1 tablespoon honey
80 ml (2½ fl oz/⅓ cup) olive oil
500 g (1 lb 2 oz) jap or butternut
   pumpkin (squash)
400 g (14 oz) fresh chestnuts, peeled,
   or 200 g (7 oz) frozen peeled
   chestnuts, thawed
100 g (3½ oz) rocket (arugula)

**ORANGE AND SHERRY VINEGAR
   DRESSING**
80 ml (2½ fl oz/⅓ cup) extra virgin
   olive oil
1½ tablespoons sherry vinegar
1 teaspoon finely grated orange rind
1 garlic clove, crushed

• Preheat the oven to 180°C (350°F/Gas 4). Peel and trim the parsnips, then trim tips. Cut the parsnips into quarters lengthways and place in a large roasting tin. Cut the pears in half down the middle, remove the core, then cut each half into three wedges. Place in the roasting tin with the parsnip. Scatter with half the thyme sprigs, then drizzle with half the honey and 2½ tablespoons of the olive oil. Season to taste with sea salt and freshly ground black pepper.

• Peel the pumpkin, remove the seeds, then cut the flesh into 1 cm (½ inch)-thick slices. Place in another roasting tin, scatter with the remaining thyme sprigs and drizzle with the remaining honey and oil. Season to taste.

• Bake the parsnip, pear and pumpkin for 20 minutes. Turn over and roast for a further 10 minutes, or until the pumpkin is tender. Set the pumpkin aside.

● Add the chestnuts to the parsnip and pear and roast for a further 15 minutes, or until all are tender and golden. Remove from the oven and allow to cool slightly.

● Meanwhile, place the orange and sherry vinegar dressing ingredients in a small bowl and whisk together well.

● In a large mixing bowl, combine the pumpkin, parsnip, pear, chestnuts and rocket. Drizzle the dressing over and toss gently to combine.

● Arrange on a platter, or divide among serving bowls or plates and serve.

ASPARAGUS, BEAN AND EGG SALAD

preparation time 30 minutes
cooking time 10 minutes
serves 4

2 handfuls coriander (cilantro) leaves,
    including roots
1½ teaspoons finely grated ginger
2 tablespoons sweet chilli sauce
2 teaspoons soy sauce
finely grated rind and juice of 1 lime
185 ml (6 fl oz/¾ cup) light coconut
    milk
1 teaspoon chilli flakes, or to taste
8 asparagus spears (about 1 bunch),
    trimmed

200 g (7 oz/1⅔ cups) green beans or
    sugar snap peas, trimmed
225 g (8 oz/2½ cups) bean sprouts,
    tails trimmed
1 small red onion, very thinly sliced
2 hard-boiled eggs, peeled and cut
    into wedges
50 g (2 oz/⅓ cup) coarsely chopped
    roasted peanuts (optional)

● Remove the roots from the coriander and wash well, reserving the remaining coriander. Chop the roots finely, then combine in a food processor with the ginger, sweet chilli sauce, soy sauce, lime rind and juice, coconut milk and chilli flakes. Process until a smooth dressing forms, then season to taste with sea salt and freshly ground black pepper. Set aside.

● Bring a saucepan of salted water to the boil. Cut the asparagus in half lengthways, then add to the boiling water with the beans, cover and cook for 2–3 minutes or until tender. Drain well, then rinse the vegetables under cold running water until cool. Drain well and pat dry using paper towels.

● Trim the long stems from the coriander, then combine the coriander sprigs with the cooked vegetables, bean sprouts and onion in a large bowl. Add the dressing and toss gently to combine. Divide the salad among plates or bowls, scatter over the egg wedges and peanuts, if using, and serve immediately.

FARFALLE SALAD WITH SUN-DRIED TOMATOES AND SPINACH

preparation time 20 minutes
cooking time 15 minutes
serves 6

500 g (1 lb 2 oz) farfalle or spiral
   pasta
3 spring onions (scallions)
50 g (2 oz) sun-dried tomatoes, cut
   into strips
1 kg (2 lb 4 oz) English spinach, stalks
   trimmed and leaves shredded

50 g (2 oz/$\frac{1}{3}$ cup) pine nuts, toasted
1 tablespoon chopped oregano
60 ml (2 fl oz/$\frac{1}{4}$ cup) olive oil
1 teaspoon sliced chilli
1 garlic clove, crushed

● Cook the pasta in a large saucepan of rapidly boiling salted water until al dente. Drain, rinse under cold water and drain again. Allow to cool and transfer to a large salad bowl.

● Trim the spring onions and thinly slice diagonally. Add to the pasta with the tomato, spinach, pine nuts and oregano.

● To make the dressing, combine the oil, chilli, garlic and salt and pepper in a small screw-top jar and shake well. Pour the dressing over the top of the salad and toss to combine.

BEAN, ASPARAGUS AND POTATO SALAD WITH SMOKED PAPRIKA ROMESCO

preparation time 40 minutes

cooking time 35 minutes

serves 6

600 g (1 lb 5 oz) kipfler (fingerling) or
  other waxy potatoes, scrubbed
250 g (9 oz) baby green beans,
  trimmed
250 g (9 oz) sugar snap peas,
  trimmed
2 bunches (350 g/12 oz) asparagus
  (about 18 spears), trimmed
400 g (14 oz) tin borlotti (cranberry)
  beans, rinsed and drained
80 g (3 oz/²⁄₃ cup) pitted green olives
2 large handfuls rocket (arugula)
  leaves
2½ tablespoons sherry vinegar
80 ml (2½ fl oz/⅓ cup) extra virgin
  olive oil
crusty bread, to serve

SMOKED PAPRIKA ROMESCO
2 large red capsicums (peppers)
50 g (2 oz) day-old rustic white
  bread, crusts removed
125 g (4½ oz/¾ cup) blanched
  almonds
3 garlic cloves, chopped
125 ml (4 fl oz/½ cup) undrained
  tinned chopped tomatoes
1 teaspoon smoked paprika
1 tablespoon sherry vinegar
2½ tablespoons extra virgin olive oil

- To make the smoked paprika romesco, place the whole capsicums directly over medium–low gas flames and cook, turning often, for 8–10 minutes, or until charred all over. Remove to a bowl, cover and cool. Quarter the capsicums, then using your hands, remove the seeds and blackened skin — avoid running the capsicums under water or you will lose flavour. Place the capsicums in a food processor with the remaining romesco ingredients and process until a coarse purée forms. Season to taste with sea salt and freshly ground black pepper. Transfer to a serving bowl, cover and set aside.

- Meanwhile, bring a saucepan of salted water to the boil. Add the whole potatoes and cook for 10–15 minutes, or until tender. Remove using a slotted spoon, reserving the water in the pan. Drain the potatoes well and leave to cool.

- Add the green beans to the boiling water and cook for 2–3 minutes, or until all the beans are tender. Using a slotted spoon, remove the beans to a colander and drain well, reserving the cooking water.

- Add the sugar snap peas to the boiling water and cook for 2 minutes, or until tender, then remove using a slotted spoon and drain well. Finally add the asparagus to the boiling water and cook for 2–3 minutes, or until tender. Drain well.

- Cut the potatoes into 1 cm (½ inch)-thick slices, then combine in a large bowl with the blanched vegetables, borlotti beans, olives and rocket. Add the vinegar and olive oil and toss gently to combine.

- Place the salad on a serving platter. Spoon some romesco sauce over the top. Serve with the romesco sauce passed separately, with bread on the side.

RADICCHIO SALAD WITH GRAPEFRUIT, BLUE CHEESE AND ALMONDS

preparation time 15 minutes plus 30 minutes standing
cooking time Nil
serves 4

½ red onion, thinly sliced
1 pink grapefruit
1 head of radicchio, trimmed, washed
   and drained
1 fennel bulb, trimmed, tough core
   removed, then cut in half
   lengthways and thinly sliced
50 g (2 oz/⅓ cup) smoked almonds,
   coarsely chopped
50 g (2 oz) Danish blue cheese,
   crumbled

GARLIC MUSTARD DRESSING
1 egg yolk
1 garlic clove, crushed
1 tablespoon sherry vinegar
1 tablespoon dijon mustard
100 ml (3½ fl oz) light olive oil

• Put the onion in a small bowl, cover with cold water and leave to stand for 30 minutes. Drain well and set aside.

• Remove the skin and pith from the grapefruit using a sharp serrated knife. Holding the grapefruit over a bowl to catch any juices, remove each segment by cutting close to the membrane to release the whole segment. Reserve the juice and place the segments in a large salad bowl.

• Slice or tear the radicchio into the salad bowl. Add the fennel and drained onion and gently toss to combine.

• To make the garlic mustard dressing, whisk the egg yolk, garlic, vinegar and mustard in a large bowl until well combined. Whisking constantly, add 60 ml (2 fl oz/¼ cup) of the olive oil, a teaspoon at a time. Very slowly add the remaining oil in a thin steady stream until the mixture is thickened and emulsified. Whisk in the reserved grapefruit juice and a little warm water to thin the dressing, if necessary — the dressing should have a creamy, coating consistency. Season to taste with sea salt and freshly ground black pepper.

• Drizzle the dressing over the salad and toss to coat. Scatter with the almonds and cheese, and serve.

HALOUMI WITH BEAN AND OLIVE SALAD

preparation time 15 minutes
cooking time 10 minutes
serves 6

30 g (1 oz) green beans, ends
   trimmed (about 12)
1 tablespoon small black olives
2 sun-dried tomatoes in oil, drained
   and chopped
baby oregano leaves, to serve
1 tablespoon olive oil
125 g (4½ oz) haloumi cheese, cut
   into three slices about 8 mm
   (⅜ inch) thick
lemon cheeks, to serve (optional)

LEMON AND HONEY DRESSING
2 tablespoons extra virgin olive oil
1 tablespoon lemon juice
1 tablespoon honey, warmed
1 teaspoon fresh oregano, roughly
   chopped

• To make the lemon and honey dressing, place all the ingredients in a small bowl and whisk to combine well, then season to taste with sea salt and freshly ground black pepper and set aside.

• Cook the beans in a small saucepan of boiling salted water for 2 minutes or until just tender. Drain and transfer the beans to a bowl of iced water to stop the cooking process. When the beans have cooled, drain well. Place the beans, olives and tomatoes in a bowl. Pour over a tablespoon of the dressing and toss to coat evenly. Pile the salad onto a serving plate and scatter with oregano.

• Heat the oil in a small frying pan over medium heat, add the haloumi slices and cook for 1 minute on each side or until golden. Arrange the haloumi alongside the prepared salad. Serve immediately with the dressing and lemon cheeks, if using, on the side.

WARM EGGPLANT AND FETA SALAD

preparation time 10 minutes
cooking time 5 minutes
serves 6

3 Lebanese eggplants (small
    aubergines), trimmed
1 tablespoon olive oil
1 small handful mint
35 g (1 oz/¼ cup) crumbled firm feta
    cheese

6 semi-dried (sun-blushed) tomatoes

YOGHURT DRESSING
1½ tablespoons Greek-style yoghurt
¼ teaspoon ground cumin
½ garlic clove, crushed

• To make the yoghurt dressing, combine the yoghurt, cumin, garlic and
1 teaspoon water in a small bowl and stir to combine well. Season to taste with
sea salt and freshly ground black pepper. Set aside.

• Cut the eggplants in half lengthways. Heat the oil in a heavy-based frying pan
over medium heat and cook the eggplant, cut side down, for 2 minutes, then
turn and cook for another 2 minutes or until cooked through. Place on a
serving plate, scatter over the mint, feta and tomatoes, drizzle with the yoghurt
dressing and serve immediately.

Soups & salads

93

SOBA NOODLE SALAD WITH TOFU, RADISH AND SESAME

preparation time 15 minutes
cooking time 15 minutes
serves 4

90 g (3 oz) dried soba noodles
2 tablespoons sesame seeds
250 ml (9 fl oz/1 cup) peanut oil
300 g (10½ oz) firm tofu, drained and
    cut into 2 cm (¾ inch) cubes
2 tablespoons cornflour (cornstarch)
3 radishes (about 300 g/10½ oz),
    trimmed and thinly sliced
100 g (3½ oz) snow pea (mangetout)
    sprouts, halved
1 handful coriander (cilantro) leaves
4 spring onions (scallions), thinly
    sliced on the diagonal

WASABI MISO DRESSING
1½ tablespoons white miso paste
2 tablespoons rice wine vinegar
½ teaspoon wasabi
2 teaspoons tamari
60 ml (2 fl oz/¼ cup) rice bran oil

● To make the wasabi miso dressing, whisk the miso paste, vinegar, wasabi and tamari in a small bowl to combine. Slowly whisk in the oil, then season to taste with sea salt and freshly ground black pepper. Set aside.

● Bring a large saucepan of water to the boil. Add the noodles and cook for 4 minutes, or until tender. Drain, rinse with cold water and drain again.

● Meanwhile, dry-roast the sesame seeds in a large frying pan over medium–low heat for 2 minutes, or until golden, stirring occasionally. Remove to a plate.

• Add the peanut oil to the pan. Heat the oil over medium–high heat until hot. Dust the tofu with the cornflour and fry for 2 minutes on each side, or until golden all over. Drain on paper towels.

• Place the noodles, sesame seeds and warm tofu in a large bowl with the radish, snow pea sprouts and dressing. Season to taste and gently toss.

• Divide among serving bowls and serve sprinkled with the coriander and spring onion.

ROAST ASPARAGUS AND TOFU SALAD WITH SESAME DRESSING

preparation time 15 minutes
cooking time 15 minutes
serves 4

1 tablespoon plain (all-purpose) flour
150 g (5½ oz) firm tofu, cut into
    2 cm (¾ inch) pieces
4 thick asparagus spears, trimmed
olive oil spray
1 small handful watercress sprigs
½ avocado, sliced

1 tablespoon finely shredded nori
    (about ¼ sheet), for garnish

SESAME DRESSING
1 teaspoon tamari or soy sauce
1 teaspoon sesame oil
1 teaspoon Japanese rice vinegar
2 teaspoons toasted sesame seeds

● Preheat the oven to 200°C (400°F/Gas 6). Line a baking tray with foil. To make the sesame dressing, combine the tamari, sesame oil, rice vinegar and 1 tablespoon water in a small bowl and whisk to combine well. Stir in the sesame seeds, then set aside.

● Season the flour with sea salt and freshly ground black pepper. Toss the tofu lightly in the flour, shaking off any excess. Place the asparagus and tofu on the baking tray. Spray with the oil to coat all sides of the asparagus and tofu, then roast for 12–15 minutes or until the asparagus is tender and the tofu has a crisp crust.

● Place the watercress on a serving plate. Top with the asparagus and tofu, add the avocado slices, then drizzle with the dressing, sprinkle with the nori and serve immediately.

WARM LENTIL AND RICE SALAD

preparation time 15 minutes
cooking time 40 minutes
serves 6

185 g (6½ oz/1 cup) green lentils
200 g (7 oz/1 cup) basmati rice
4 large red onions
4 garlic cloves, crushed
250 ml (9 fl oz/1 cup) olive oil
45 g (2 oz) butter

3 spring onions (scallions)
2 teaspoons ground cinnamon
2 teaspoons ground sweet paprika
2 teaspoons ground cumin
2 teaspoons ground coriander

- Cook the lentils and rice in separate saucepans of water until the grains are just tender, then drain.

- Meanwhile, finely slice the onions. Cook the onion and garlic in the oil and butter for 30 minutes, over low heat, until very soft. Chop the spring onions and set aside until ready to use.

- Stir in the cinnamon, paprika, cumin and coriander and cook for a few minutes longer.

- Combine the onion and spice mixture with the well-drained rice and lentils. Stir in the chopped spring onions until combined and add freshly ground black pepper to taste. Serve warm.

Note Do not use red lentils for this recipe as they become mushy very quickly and do not retain their shape. It is not necessary to soak the lentils prior to cooking, but they need to be rinsed thoroughly.

MIDDLE EASTERN BURGHUL SALAD

preparation time 30 minutes plus 30 minutes marinating
cooking time 15
serves 4

125 g (4½ oz/⅔ cup) fine burghul
  (bulgur)
60 ml (2 fl oz/¼ cup) lemon juice
70 g (2½ oz/½ cup) pistachio nuts
125 g (4½ oz) baby green beans,
  trimmed
1 small red onion, finely chopped
40 g (1½ oz/⅓ cup) dried cranberries

2 large handfuls flat-leaf (Italian)
  parsley, finely chopped
1 handful mint, finely chopped
1 tablespoon pomegranate molasses
1 teaspoon sugar
2 tablespoons olive oil
12 baby cos (romaine) lettuce leaves
  (about 2 heads of baby cos lettuce)
pitta bread, toasted, to serve

• Place the burghul in a small bowl. Stir in the lemon juice and 125 ml
(4 fl oz/½ cup) warm water. Leave to soak for 30 minutes, or until the burghul
is tender.

• Preheat the oven to 150°C (300°F/Gas 2). Place the pistachios on a baking
tray and roast for 10–12 minutes. Allow to cool slightly, then coarsely chop.

• Meanwhile, cook the beans in a saucepan of boiling water for 3 minutes, or
until tender-crisp and bright green. Drain and refresh under cold running water
until cooled. Drain and slice thinly, then set aside.

• Place the burghul, pistachios, beans, onion, cranberries and herbs in a large
bowl. Mix together the pomegranate molasses, sugar and olive oil, then drizzle
over the burghul mixture and toss gently to combine.

• Arrange three lettuce leaves on each serving plate. Divide the burghul
mixture among the leaves and serve with pitta bread.

MUSHROOM SALAD WITH CIABATTA CROUTONS AND MINT SALSA VERDE

preparation time 15 minutes
cooking time 30 minutes
serves 4

12 medium mushroom flats

2 garlic cloves, crushed

80 ml (2½ fl oz/⅓ cup) olive oil

100 g (3½ oz) ciabatta bread, torn
into 1 cm (½ inch) chunks

150 g (5½ oz) rocket (arugula),
trimmed and coarsely chopped

50 g (2 oz/½ cup) shaved parmesan
cheese

2 tablespoons lemon juice

MINT SALSA VERDE

1 French shallot, finely chopped

2 teaspoons sherry vinegar

60 ml (2 fl oz/¼ cup) extra virgin olive
oil

1 tablespoon chopped mint leaves

2½ tablespoons chopped flat-leaf
(Italian) parsley

● Preheat the oven to 180°C (350°F/Gas 4). Combine the mint salsa verde
ingredients in a bowl. Mix together and set aside. Place the mushrooms in a
single layer in a roasting tin. Combine the garlic with half the olive oil, then
drizzle over the mushrooms. Season to taste with sea salt and freshly ground
black pepper.

● Place the bread on a baking tray in a single layer and drizzle with the
remaining oil. Bake the bread and the mushrooms for 20 minutes, or until the
mushrooms are tender. Remove the mushrooms from the oven and set aside.
Bake the bread for a further 10 minutes, or until golden and crisp. Remove
from the oven. Place the rocket, parmesan, lemon juice and ciabatta croutons
in a bowl. Add the salsa verde and mix well. Arrange the mushrooms in shallow
serving bowls. Pile the rocket mixture over the top and serve.

Soups & salads

Mains

Here are curries and stews,
and pasta, grain and rice dishes
aromatic with herbs and spices.

EGGPLANT CURRY

preparation time 20 minutes
cooking time 45 minutes
serves 4

400 ml (14 fl oz) tin coconut cream
9 Japanese eggplants (aubergines),
    about 700 g (1 lb 9 oz), cut into
    2 cm (¾ inch)-thick rounds
1 teaspoon ground turmeric
2 tablespoons peanut oil
400 g (14 oz) tin chopped tomatoes
6 kaffir lime leaves, finely shredded,
    plus extra, to garnish
2 tablespoons soy sauce
1 tablespoon finely grated palm
    sugar (jaggery)
steamed rice, to serve
lime wedges, to serve

CURRY PASTE

3 garlic cloves, chopped
3 red Asian shallots, chopped
2–4 small red chillies, or to taste,
    seeded and chopped
2 lemongrass stems, white part only,
    finely chopped
1 tablespoon coarsely grated or finely
    chopped fresh ginger
4 coriander (cilantro) roots, finely
    chopped

• Combine the curry paste ingredients in a food processor or blender and
process until a smooth paste forms, adding a little water if needed.

• Place 200 ml (7 fl oz) of the coconut cream in a wok over low heat. Bring to
a simmer and cook for 10 minutes, or until the oil starts to separate out.
Increase the heat to medium, add the curry paste and cook for 5 minutes, or
until aromatic. Transfer the mixture to a small bowl and set aside. Wipe the
wok clean.

• Place the eggplant in a large bowl, add the turmeric and toss to coat. Reheat
the wok over high heat and add the oil. When the oil is hot, add the eggplant
and stir-fry for 4–5 minutes, or until browned and softened.

- Add the curry mixture and cook, stirring, for a further 2 minutes, or until aromatic. Stir in the tomato, lime leaves and remaining coconut cream, then cover and simmer for 15 minutes, or until the eggplant is very tender.

- Remove the lid. Stir in the soy sauce and palm sugar and simmer, stirring occasionally, for 1–2 minutes, or until the sugar has dissolved.

- Serve the curry on a bed of steamed rice, garnished with extra shredded lime leaves, and with lime wedges on the side.

Mains

CAULIFLOWER AND WHITE BEAN KORMA

preparation time 20 minutes
cooking time 35 minutes
serves 4

60 ml (2 fl oz/¼ cup) peanut oil
500 g (1 lb 2 oz/4 cups) cauliflower
    florets (from about ½ head of
    cauliflower)
1 brown onion, finely chopped
4 vine-ripened tomatoes (about
    500 g/1 lb 2 oz), finely chopped
100 ml (3½ fl oz) vegetable stock
12 curry leaves, plus extra, to garnish
120 g (4 oz/¾ cup) roasted cashew
    nuts, coarsely chopped
400 g (14 oz) tin white beans (such
    as cannellini), rinsed and drained
80 ml (2½ fl oz/⅓ cup) cream
warmed naan bread, to serve
steamed basmati rice, to serve
lime pickle, to serve (optional)

SPICE PASTE
3 garlic cloves, crushed
2 teaspoons grated fresh ginger
2 teaspoons garam masala
1 teaspoon ground turmeric
1 teaspoon ground cumin
1 teaspoon ground coriander
1 teaspoon chilli powder
1 teaspoon sea salt

- Heat half the oil in a large heavy-based frying pan over medium–high heat. Add the cauliflower and cook, stirring, for 5 minutes, or until golden. Transfer the cauliflower to a plate.

- Heat the remaining oil in the pan. Add the onion and cook over medium heat, stirring occasionally, for 8 minutes, or until softened.

- Meanwhile, to make the spice paste, combine all the ingredients in a small food processor and blend until a paste forms.

- Add the spice paste to the onion and cook, stirring, for 1 minute, or until aromatic.

- Stir in the tomato, stock, curry leaves, cashews, beans and sautéed cauliflower. Bring to a simmer, then reduce the heat to low. Cover and cook for 10–15 minutes, or until the cauliflower is tender. Stir in the cream and cook for 1–2 minutes, or until heated through.

- Ladle the curry into serving bowls and garnish with the extra curry leaves. Serve with naan bread and steamed rice, and lime pickle if desired.

Mains

GREEN VEGETABLE CURRY

preparation time 20 minutes
cooking time 35 minutes
serves 4

1 tablespoon vegetable oil
2 tablespoons vegetarian Thai green
   curry paste
350 ml (12 fl oz) coconut milk
2 potatoes, peeled and cut into 2 cm
   (¾ inch) cubes
3 Japanese eggplants (aubergines),
   cut into 2 cm (¾ inch)-thick rounds
½ butternut pumpkin (squash), about
   400 g (14 oz), peeled and cut into
   2 cm (¾ inch) cubes

1 small sweet potato (about 400 g/
   14 oz), peeled and cut into 2 cm
   (¾ inch) cubes
7 kaffir lime leaves, 5 torn and
   2 finely shredded
1 tablespoon soy sauce
1 tablespoon lime juice
40 g (1½ oz/1/4 cup) cashew nuts,
   toasted and coarsely chopped
1 small handful coriander (cilantro)
   leaves
1 small handful mint leaves, shredded
steamed jasmine rice, to serve

● Heat the oil in a wok over medium heat. Add the curry paste and cook, stirring, for 2–3 minutes, or until fragrant. Pour in the coconut milk and stir until thoroughly combined. Simmer for 3 minutes, or until the oil starts to separate out.

● Add the potato and eggplant to the wok and cook, stirring occasionally, for 10 minutes. Add the pumpkin and sweet potato and cook for a further 10 minutes, or until all the vegetables are tender.

● Add the torn lime leaves, soy sauce and lime juice and heat through.

● Ladle the curry into serving bowls. Garnish with the cashews, coriander, mint and shredded lime leaves and serve with steamed jasmine rice.

SPINACH DHAL

preparation time 15 minutes
cooking time 1 hour 10 minutes
serves 4

1½ tablespoons vegetable oil
1 onion, finely chopped
1 garlic clove, crushed
½ teaspoon ground turmeric
½ teaspoon chilli powder
1 teaspoon cumin seeds
1 teaspoon mustard seeds
330 g (11½ oz/1½ cups) yellow split
   peas, rinsed and drained

250 g (9 oz) packet frozen spinach,
   thawed, then squeezed as dry as
   possible
1 small handful coriander (cilantro)
   leaves, chopped
2 teaspoons garam masala
1½ tablespoons lemon juice
mango chutney, to serve
Greek-style yoghurt, to serve
warm naan bread, to serve

● Heat the oil in a flameproof casserole dish over medium heat. Add the onion and sauté for 5 minutes, or until softened. Add the garlic, turmeric, chilli powder, cumin seeds and mustard seeds and stir for a further 2 minutes, or until the spices are fragrant and the mustard seeds start to pop.

● Add the split peas and 875 ml (30 fl oz/3½ cups) cold water. Bring to the boil, then cover and simmer, stirring occasionally, for 50–60 minutes, or until the split peas are tender and the liquid is almost absorbed.

● Remove the dhal from the heat, then stir in the spinach, coriander, garam masala and lemon juice. Season to taste with sea salt and freshly ground black pepper. Serve with chutney, yoghurt and warm naan bread.

Mains

DRY POTATO CURRY WITH EGG AND PEAS

preparation time 25 minutes
cooking time 45 minutes
serves 4

4 eggs
220 g (8 oz/1 cup) brown rice
1 tablespoon vegetable oil
2 teaspoons brown mustard seeds
40 g (1½ oz) butter
2 brown onions, thinly sliced
2 garlic cloves, chopped
2 teaspoons grated fresh ginger
1 green chilli, chopped
2 teaspoons ground turmeric
1 teaspoon ground cumin
1 teaspoon garam masala
750 g (1 lb 10 oz) waxy potatoes,
    peeled and cut into 3 cm (1¼ inch)
    chunks

100 g (3½ oz/⅔ cup) frozen peas,
    thawed
2 tablespoons lemon juice
1 small handful mint leaves
2 tablespoons mango chutney

MINT AND GINGER RAITA

125 g (4½ oz/½ cup) Greek-style
    yoghurt
1 Lebanese (short) cucumber, peeled,
    seeds removed and coarsely
    grated
1 garlic clove, crushed
½ teaspoon grated fresh ginger
1 small handful mint leaves, finely
    chopped

● To make the mint and ginger raita, place all the ingredients in a small bowl. Mix together well and season to taste with sea salt. Cover and refrigerate until serving time.

● Bring a small saucepan of cold water to the boil over medium heat. Add the eggs, reduce the heat to low and simmer for 10 minutes. Remove the eggs and place in a bowl of cold water until cooled. Drain the eggs, then peel, cut into halves and set aside.

• Place the rice in a saucepan. Add 750 ml (26 fl oz/3 cups) water and bring to a simmer. Cook, adding more water if necessary, for 20–30 minutes, or until tender. Drain well, cover and keep warm

• Meanwhile, heat the oil in a frying pan. Add the mustard seeds and cook over medium heat until the seeds start to pop. Reduce the heat to low, then add the butter and onion and cook, stirring, for 5 minutes, or until the onion has softened. Add the garlic, ginger, chilli, spices and potato, stirring to coat in the spice mix. Pour in 125 ml (4 fl oz/½ cup) water, then cover and simmer over low heat for 25 minutes, or until the potato is just tender.

• Stir in the peas and lemon juice and cook for 3 minutes, or until the peas are heated through. Stir in the mint and season to taste with sea salt and freshly ground black pepper.

• Divide the rice among serving plates or bowls. Top with the curry and garnish with the egg halves. Serve topped with a dollop of the mint and ginger raita, with the mango chutney on the side.

Mains

THAI VEGETABLE RED CURRY

preparation time 20 minutes
cooking time 35 minutes
serves 4

1 tablespoon Thai red curry paste
2 garlic cloves, chopped
2 red Asian shallots, chopped
1 x 270 ml (9½ fl oz) tin coconut
    cream
1 x 400 ml (14 fl oz) tin coconut milk
250 ml (9 fl oz/1 cup) vegetable stock
2 desiree potatoes, peeled and cut
    into 2 cm (¾ inch) chunks
150 g (5½ oz) sweet potato, peeled
    and cut into 2 cm (¾ inch) chunks
400 g (14 oz) broccoli, cut into florets

1 red capsicum (pepper), cut into
    strips 1 cm (½ inch) wide
1 carrot, cut in half lengthways,
    then thinly sliced
6 small button mushrooms
1 tablespoon soy sauce
1 tablespoon lime juice
1 tablespoon shaved palm sugar
    (jaggery)
1 small handful coriander (cilantro)
    leaves, chopped
chopped toasted peanuts, to serve
steamed jasmine rice, to serve
lime halves, to serve

- Place the curry paste, garlic and shallots in a food processor and blend until a smooth paste forms. Set aside.

- Pour the coconut cream into a wok or large saucepan and bring to the boil over medium heat. Reduce the heat to low and simmer for 10 minutes, or until the oil starts to separate from the cream and the surface appears shiny. Add the curry paste mixture and cook, stirring, for 3 minutes, or until fragrant

- Pour in the coconut milk and stock and bring to a simmer. Add the potato and sweet potato, then cover and cook over medium–low heat for 10 minutes. Add the broccoli, capsicum, carrot and mushrooms. Cover and cook for 5 minutes, or until the vegetables are tender, tossing the wok occasionally.

• Stir in the soy sauce, lime juice, palm sugar and coriander and cook for a further 3 minutes.

• Sprinkle with chopped toasted peanuts. Serve with steamed jasmine rice and lime halves.

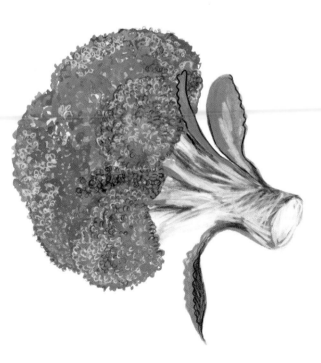

GREEK BEAN STEW WITH FRIED HALOUMI

preparation time 25 minutes
cooking time 2 hours
serves 4

500 g (1 lb 2 oz/2½ cups) dried
   white beans, such as cannellini or
   great northern beans
80 ml (2½ fl oz/⅓ cup) extra virgin
   olive oil
2 large onions, chopped
3 garlic cloves, finely chopped
6 celery stalks, thinly sliced
2 large carrots, thinly sliced
2 tablespoons tomato paste
   (concentrated purée)
2 teaspoons ground allspice

3 dried Greek oregano sprigs, or
   1 tablespoon dried oregano
500 ml (17 fl oz/2 cups) dry red wine
2 x 800 g (1 lb 12 oz) tins chopped
   tomatoes
90 g (3 oz/¼ cup) honey
2½ tablespoons red wine vinegar,
   or to taste
1 large handful flat-leaf (Italian)
   parsley, chopped, plus extra, to
   garnish
200 g (7 oz) haloumi, cut into wide
   slices 1 cm (½ inch) thick

• Soak the beans in cold water overnight, then drain well. Transfer to a large saucepan, cover with cold water and bring to a simmer over medium heat. Skim off any froth that rises to the surface, then simmer for 30 minutes, or until the beans are half cooked. Drain well.

• Rinse the pan and wipe dry. Heat about 2½ tablespoons of the olive oil in the pan over medium heat. Add the onion and garlic and sauté for 5−6 minutes, or until the onion has softened.

• Add the celery and carrot and sauté for 6−7 minutes, or until the vegetables have softened. Add the tomato paste and allspice and cook for 1−2 minutes, then add the oregano, wine, tomatoes, honey, vinegar and beans. Mix well, then stir in just enough water to cover the beans.

• Bring the mixture to a gentle simmer, then reduce the heat to low. Cover and cook, stirring occasionally, for 1 hour, or until the beans are very tender. Remove the stems of the dried oregano sprigs, if using. Stir in the parsley and season to taste with sea salt and freshly ground black pepper. Keep warm.

• Heat the remaining olive oil in a large frying pan over medium heat. Fry the haloumi for 2 minutes on each side, or until light golden and heated through.

• Ladle 2 spoonfuls of the bean stew into serving bowls. Top with the haloumi, sprinkle with extra parsley and serve.

Mains

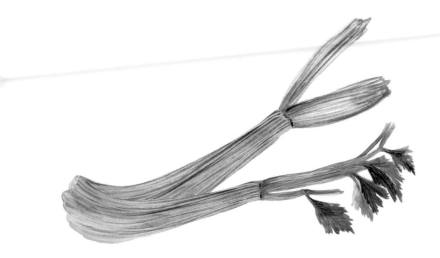

PERSIAN VEGETABLE AND FRUIT STEW

preparation time 25 minutes
cooking time 1 hour 20 minutes
serves 4–6

2 tablespoons vegetable oil
2 brown onions, finely chopped
3 garlic cloves, finely chopped
2 celery stalks, finely chopped
2 carrots, sliced into 2 cm
 (¾ inch)-thick rounds
400 g (14 oz) kipfler (fingerling) or
 other waxy potatoes, scrubbed and
 sliced into 2 cm (¾ inch)-thick
 rounds
1 turnip (about 350 g/12 oz), peeled
 and cut into 2 cm (¾ inch) cubes
2 large granny smith apples, peeled,
 cored and chopped
2 teaspoons ground turmeric
1 handful flat-leaf (Italian) parsley,
 chopped

1 handful coriander (cilantro) leaves,
 chopped, plus extra, to garnish
100 g (3½ oz/½ cup) pitted prunes,
 chopped
100 g (3½ oz/½ cup) dried apricots,
 chopped
1.25 litres (44 fl oz/5 cups) vegetable
 stock, approximately

SAFFRON RICE
30 g (1 oz) butter
400 g (14 oz/2 cups) basmati rice,
 rinsed well and drained
a large pinch of saffron threads

● Heat the oil in a large flameproof casserole dish over medium heat. Add the
onion, garlic and celery and cook, stirring, for 10–15 minutes.

● Add the carrot, potato, turnip, apple, turmeric and herbs and cook for
2 minutes, then add the prunes and apricots and enough of the stock to just
cover the mixture. Bring to the boil, cover and reduce the heat to a gentle
simmer. Cook for 40 minutes, then remove the lid and cook for a further
10–20 minutes, or until the vegetables are tender and the stew is rich and
thick. Season to taste with sea salt and freshly ground black pepper.

• Meanwhile, make the saffron rice. Melt the butter in a saucepan over medium heat. Add the rice and saffron and cook, stirring, for 2–3 minutes, or until the rice is heated through. Add 750 ml (26 fl oz/3 cups) water and quickly bring just to a simmer, then cover, reduce the heat to low and cook for 12 minutes, or until the water is absorbed. Remove from the heat and leave to stand, covered, for 5 minutes, then fluff the grains up with a fork.

• Divide the rice among serving bowls and spoon the stew over. Garnish with the extra coriander and serve.

Mains

TUNISIAN VEGETABLE STEW WITH LEMON PICKLE

preparation time 45 minutes
cooking time 1 hour 20 minutes
serves 4–6

2 tablespoons olive oil
1 large brown onion, finely sliced
3 garlic cloves, finely chopped
2 teaspoons ground coriander
1 teaspoon ground turmeric
½ teaspoon ground cinnamon
1–2 tablespoons tomato paste
   (concentrated purée)
750 ml (26 fl oz/3 cups) vegetable
   stock
2 potatoes (about 400 g/14 oz),
   peeled and cut into 2 cm (¾ inch)
   chunks
100 g (3½ oz/1⅓ cups) thinly sliced
   cabbage
150 g (5½ oz/1 cup) fresh pitted
   dates, chopped
150 g (5½ oz/1¼ cups) small
   cauliflower florets
200 g (7 oz) green beans, trimmed
   and halved diagonally
steamed couscous, to serve
1 large handful coriander (cilantro)
   leaves, chopped, to serve (optional)
35 g (1 oz/¼ cup) chopped pistachio
   nuts, to serve (optional)

LEMON PICKLE

3 lemons (about 450g/1 lb)
1 tablespoon olive oil
1 brown onion, thinly sliced
1 tablespoon finely grated fresh
   ginger
2 garlic cloves, crushed
1 teaspoon yellow mustard seeds
½ teaspoon ground allspice
1 teaspoon ground coriander
½ teaspoon hot chilli powder
200 ml (7 fl oz) cider vinegar
1½ teaspoons sea salt
55 g (2 oz/¼ cup) sugar

- To make the lemon pickle, cut the lemons in half widthways, juice the lemons, then strain the juice and set aside. Cut the lemon halves in half again, then remove all the flesh and white pith using a small, sharp knife, leaving just the yellow skin. Slice the skin into very thin strips and set aside.

- Heat the olive oil in a heavy-based saucepan over medium–low heat. Add the onion and cook, stirring, for 8 minutes, or until softened but not coloured. Add the ginger, garlic and spices and cook for a further 30 seconds. Pour in the vinegar, lemon juice and 125 ml (4 fl oz/½ cup) water, then stir in the salt. Bring to the boil, reduce the heat to a gentle simmer and cook, stirring occasionally, for 1 hour, or until the lemon skins are very tender. Increase the heat to medium–high and stir in the sugar. Cook for a further 10 minutes.

- Meanwhile, prepare the stew. Heat the olive oil in a heavy-based saucepan over medium–low heat. Add the onion and cook, stirring, for 8 minutes, or until softened. Add the garlic, spices and tomato paste and stir for 1 minute.

- Pour in the stock and add the potato. Bring to the boil, reduce the heat to a gentle simmer, then cover and cook for 20 minutes, or until the potato is just tender. Add the cabbage, dates, cauliflower and beans. Cover and cook for a further 10–15 minutes.

- Divide the stew among serving bowls. Serve with the pickle and couscous on the side, and the coriander and pistachios to sprinkle over, if desired.

Mains

SILVERBEET, CHICKPEA AND ALMOND TAGINE

preparation time 30 minutes
cooking time 45 minutes
serves 4

2 tablespoons olive oil
2 red onions, thinly sliced
2 garlic cloves, crushed
2 teaspoons ground cumin
1½ teaspoons ground cinnamon
½ teaspoon chilli powder
350 g (12 oz) butternut pumpkin
   (squash), peeled, seeded and cut
   into 2 cm (¾ inch) wedges
2 x 400 g (14 oz) tins chopped
   tomatoes
400 g (14 oz) tin chickpeas, rinsed
   and drained

1 small cauliflower, cut into florets
1 kg (2 lb 4 oz/1 bunch) silverbeet
   (Swiss chard), washed, stems
   trimmed and chopped
1 tablespoon finely chopped
   preserved lemon rind, or
   2 teaspoons finely grated
   lemon rind
couscous, to serve
1 handful coriander (cilantro) leaves
50 g (2 oz/⅓ cup) whole roasted
   almonds, roughly chopped
lemon wedges, to serve

• Heat the olive oil in a large heavy-based saucepan over medium heat. Add the onion and sauté for 7–10 minutes, or until translucent. Add the garlic and spices and cook for a further 30 seconds, or until fragrant.

• Add the pumpkin, tomatoes, chickpeas and 250 ml (9 fl oz/1 cup) water. Cover, bring to the boil, then reduce the heat to medium–low and cook for 20 minutes, stirring occasionally.

• Add the cauliflower and cook for a further 10 minutes, or until the vegetables are tender.

• Stir in the silverbeet and preserved lemon and simmer gently for 3 minutes. Season to taste with sea salt and freshly ground black pepper.

• Spoon the tagine into serving bowls and sprinkle with the coriander and almonds. Serve with couscous and lemon wedges.

MOROCCAN RATATOUILLE

preparation time 20 minutes
cooking time 4 hours 20 minutes
serves 4

80 ml (2½ fl oz/⅓ cup) olive oil, approximately

2 large red onions, cut into 2 cm (¾ inch) chunks

2 eggplants (aubergine), about 450 g (1 lb) each, trimmed and cut into 2.5 cm (1 inch) chunks

2 large red capsicums (peppers), trimmed, seeded and chopped into 2.5 cm (1 inch) chunks

2 tablespoons Moroccan spice mix

2 x 400 g (14 oz) tins chopped tomatoes

2 tablespoons tomato paste (concentrated purée)

400 g (14 oz) tin chickpeas, rinsed and drained

750 g (1 lb 10 oz) butternut pumpkin (squash), peeled, seeded and cut into 3 cm (1¼ inch) chunks

2 tablespoons lemon juice

2½ teaspoons honey

110 g (4 oz/⅔ cup) pimento-stuffed green olives

2 tablespoons chopped coriander (cilantro)

250 g (9 oz/1 cup) Greek yoghurt

1 tablespoon chopped mint

steamed rice, to serve

harissa, to serve

● Heat 1 tablespoon of the olive oil in a large heavy-based frying pan over medium heat. Add the onion and cook, tossing occasionally, for 4 minutes, or until the onion starts to soften and brown. Transfer the onion to a slow cooker.

● Heat another 1 tablespoon of oil in the pan and add half the eggplant. Cook for 2 minutes on each side, or until the eggplant has softened slightly and is light golden, adding a little more oil as necessary. Add to the slow cooker.

● Heat another tablespoon of oil in the pan, then cook the remaining eggplant in the same way. Add to the slow cooker.

● Heat another tablespoon oil in the pan, then add the capsicum and cook for 3–4 minutes, or until it starts to soften and brown, turning often. Add the Moroccan spice mix and mix to combine well. Cook, stirring, for 30 seconds, or until fragrant, then add 1 tin of tomatoes, stirring to loosen any stuck-on bits from the bottom of the pan.

● Transfer the mixture to the slow cooker. Add the remaining tomatoes, the tomato paste and the chickpeas and stir to combine well. Arrange the pumpkin on top of the mixture. Cover and cook on low for 4 hours, or until the vegetables are very tender but still holding their shape.

● Gently stir in the lemon juice, honey, olives and coriander. Season to taste with sea salt and freshly ground black pepper.

● Combine the yoghurt and mint. Serve the ratatouille on a bed of steamed rice, with the minted yoghurt and harissa.

Note *This dish can be cooked in a casserole dish in the oven; you will need to add extra liquid.*

Mains

BAKED VEGETABLES WITH HALOUMI

preparation time 20 minutes
cooking time 1 hour 20 minutes
serves 6

1 fennel bulb (about 450 g/1 lb),
   trimmed, tough cores removed,
   then cut into 2 cm (¾ inch) wedges
2 small carrots, quartered lengthways
1 yellow capsicum (pepper), cut into
   1 cm (½ inch)-thick strips
1 red onion, cut into 2 cm (¾ inch)
   wedges
6 whole garlic cloves
2 teaspoons ground coriander
1 teaspoon chilli flakes
½ teaspoon ground allspice
1½ teaspoons sea salt
2½ tablespoons olive oil, plus extra,
   for drizzling
2 zucchini (courgettes), cut into 1 cm
   (½ inch)-thick rounds

1 tablespoon lemon juice
400 g (14 oz) tin chickpeas, rinsed
   and drained
250 g (9 oz) haloumi cheese, cut into
   1 cm (½ inch)-thick slices
1 handful coarsely chopped flat-leaf
   (Italian) parsley
Greek-style yoghurt, to serve

TOMATO SAUCE

1½ tablespoons olive oil
1 brown onion, finely chopped
2 garlic cloves, finely chopped
800 g (1 lb 12 oz) tin chopped
   tomatoes
1 teaspoon thyme leaves

● Preheat the oven to 180°C (350°F/Gas 4). Line two baking trays with baking paper, allowing the paper to overhang the edges a little.

● In a large bowl, combine the fennel, carrot, capsicum, onion, garlic, spices, salt and the olive oil, tossing to coat the vegetables. Spread the vegetables on the baking trays, then cover tightly with foil and bake for 30 minutes. Remove and discard the foil. Add the zucchini to the baking trays and sprinkle with the lemon juice. Toss to combine, then bake for a further 25 minutes.

● Remove the vegetables from the oven, toss gently again and add the chickpeas and haloumi. Drizzle with some extra olive oil and toss gently. Bake for a final 25 minutes, or until the vegetables are very tender and the haloumi is golden and heated through.

● Meanwhile, make the tomato sauce. In a saucepan, heat the olive oil over medium–high heat. Add the onion and cook, stirring, for 8 minutes, or until softened. Add the garlic and cook for a further 2 minutes. Add the tomatoes and thyme and simmer for 20 minutes, or until the sauce has reduced by half. Season to taste with sea salt and freshly ground black pepper.

● Serve the vegetables topped with the tomato sauce and sprinkled with the parsley. Accompany with the yoghurt.

VEGETARIAN CHILLI BEANS

preparation time 20 minutes
cooking time 4 hours
serves 4

1 onion, chopped
1 red capsicum (pepper), trimmed,
   seeded and chopped
400 g (14 oz) tin chopped tomatoes
2 x 400 g (14 oz) tins red kidney
   beans, rinsed and drained
1 tablespoon tomato paste
   (concentrated purée)
3 teaspoons ground coriander
2 teaspoons ground cumin
$\frac{1}{2}$ teaspoon chilli powder
2 garlic cloves, crushed
2 bay leaves
125 ml (4 fl oz/$\frac{1}{2}$ cup) vegetable
   stock
400 g (14 oz/2 cups) basmati rice
90 g (3 oz/$\frac{1}{3}$ cup) sour cream
1 small handful coriander (cilantro)
   sprigs
flour tortillas, to serve

AVOCADO SALSA

1 avocado, peeled and diced
2 tablespoons lemon juice
1 roma (plum) tomato, seeded and
   diced
$\frac{1}{2}$ red onion, thinly sliced

- Place the onion, capsicum, tomatoes, beans, tomato paste, coriander, cumin, chilli powder, garlic and bay leaves in a slow cooker. Pour in the stock and stir to combine well. Cover and cook for 4 hours on low.

- Meanwhile, near serving time, prepare the rice. Rinse the rice under cold running water until the water runs clear. Place the rice and 375 ml (13 fl oz/ 1½ cups) cold water in a large saucepan, then cover and cook over low heat for 20–25 minutes, or until the rice is tender.

- To make the avocado salsa, put all the ingredients in a bowl and stir to combine. Season to taste with sea salt and freshly ground black pepper. Cover and refrigerate until required.

- Spoon the chilli beans into serving bowls. Top with a dollop of the sour cream and garnish with the coriander sprigs. Serve with the rice, salsa and tortillas.

Note *This dish can be cooked in a casserole dish in the oven; you will need to add extra liquid.*

Mains

VEGETABLE SKEWERS WITH PARSNIP SKORDALIA

preparation time 20 minutes plus 30 minutes soaking
cooking time 30 minutes
serves 4

2 red capsicums (peppers), cut into
    2 cm (¾ inch) pieces
3 Japanese eggplants (aubergines),
    cut into 1 cm (½ inch)-thick rounds
3 zucchini (courgettes), cut into 1 cm
    (½ inch)-thick rounds
2 tablespoons olive oil
½ teaspoon dried oregano
350 g (12 oz) haloumi cheese, cut
    into 2 cm (¾ inch) cubes
chopped flat-leaf (Italian) parsley,
    to garnish
lemon wedges, to serve

PARSNIP SKORDALIA
500 g (1 lb 2 oz) parsnips, peeled,
    core removed and chopped
300 g (10½ oz) sebago or other
    floury potatoes, peeled and
    chopped
60 ml (2 fl oz/¼ cup) olive oil
2 tablespoons lemon juice
3–4 garlic cloves, crushed

- Soak 12 bamboo skewers in cold water for 30 minutes to prevent scorching.

- To make the parsnip skordalia, place the parsnip and potato in a saucepan of boiling water and cook for 15–20 minutes, or until very tender. Drain well, then mash until smooth. (Do not use a food processor to mash the mixture or the potato will become gluey.) Transfer the mixture to a bowl and stir in the olive oil, lemon juice and garlic until well combined. Cover to keep warm.

- Meanwhile, preheat the grill (broiler) to medium–high. Place the capsicum, eggplant and zucchini in a bowl. Add the olive oil and oregano and toss to coat the vegetables.

- Thread the vegetables and haloumi alternately onto the skewers. Grill the skewers, turning regularly, for 10–12 minutes, or until the vegetables are tender and the haloumi is lightly golden.

- Divide the warm skordalia among serving plates or shallow bowls. Top with the skewers. Garnish with parsley and serve immediately, with lemon wedges.

Mains

CARAMELISED ONION TARTE TATIN

preparation time 35 minutes plus 20 minutes cooling
cooking time 2 hours 10 minutes
serves 4

4 large brown onions (about 250 g/
    9 oz each)
2 tablespoons olive oil
1½ tablespoons rosemary
20 g (¾ oz) butter, diced
1½ tablespoons good-quality
    balsamic vinegar
1 sheet frozen puff pastry, thawed
    and chilled

**WATERCRESS, WALNUT AND
GOAT'S CHEESE SALAD**
2 handfuls picked watercress sprigs
60 g (2 oz/½ cup) coarsely
    chopped walnuts
1 tablespoon balsamic vinegar
50 ml (1½ fl oz) extra virgin olive oil
100 g (3½ oz) soft goat's cheese,
    coarsely crumbled

● Preheat the oven to 150°C (300°F/Gas 2). Line a large baking tray with baking paper.

● Keeping the skin on, remove a thin slice from the top and root ends of the onions. Slice the onions into 1.5 cm (⅝ inch)-thick rounds and place on the baking tray in a single layer. In a bowl, mix together the olive oil and 1 tablespoon rosemary and season with sea salt and freshly ground black pepper. Brush the mixture over the onion rounds and bake for 1½–1¾ hours, or until the onion is well caramelised and softened, turning the slices over halfway during cooking. Remove from the oven and allow to cool for 20 minutes.

● Increase the oven temperature to 220°C (425°F/Gas 7). Peel the outside skin and any tough pieces from the onion. Place one onion round in the middle of an 18 cm (7 inch) heavy-based ovenproof frying pan, then arrange more onion rounds tightly around it. Season to taste.

- Repeat with another layer of onion and season to taste. Scatter the butter over the onion and drizzle with the vinegar.

- Cut a 22 cm (8½ inch) circle from the pastry, then place it over the onion, tucking it well down the side of the pan around the onion. Bake for 22–25 minutes, or until the pastry is golden brown and crisp.

- Near serving time, prepare the salad. Place the watercress and walnuts in a bowl. Combine the vinegar and olive oil and season to taste. Pour over the salad and gently toss. Sprinkle with the goatís cheese.

- Remove the tart from the oven and loosen the edges with a spatula. Place a plate or cutting board on top of the frying pan, then carefully invert the tart onto the plate, onion side up. Scatter the remaining rosemary over the tart.

- Cut the tart into quarters and place on serving plates. Serve with the salad.

SPICY CHICKPEA POT PIE

preparation time 30 minutes plus overnight soaking
cooking time 1¾ hours
serves 4

220 g (8 oz/1 cup) dried chickpeas
60 ml (2 fl oz/¼ cup) olive oil
1 brown onion, finely chopped
400 g (14 oz) tin chopped tomatoes
60 g (2 oz/¼ cup) tomato paste
  (concentrated purée)
¼ teaspoon ground cardamom
2 tablespoons pomegranate molasses
1 garlic clove, crushed
1 bunch (about 250 g/9 oz) English
  spinach, tough stems removed,
  leaves washed and drained
1 tablespoon chopped mint leaves
2 tablespoons chopped coriander
  (cilantro) leaves

POTATO MASH
6 Dutch cream or other waxy
  potatoes (about 700 g/1 lb 9 oz in
  total), peeled and coarsely
  chopped
1 garlic clove, crushed
60 ml (2 fl oz/¼ cup) extra virgin olive
  oil
125 ml (4 fl oz/½ cup) milk
1 tablespoon chopped flat-leaf
  (Italian) parsley
125 g (4½ oz/¾ cup) feta cheese,
  crumbled

• Place the chickpeas in a bowl. Cover with cold water and leave to soak
overnight.

• Drain the chickpeas and place in a saucepan. Add enough water to cover by
3 cm (1¼ inches). Bring to the boil over high heat, then reduce the heat and
simmer for 1 hour, or until the chickpeas are tender. Drain and set aside.

• Meanwhile, make the potato mash. Place the potato in a saucepan and cover
with water. Bring to the boil over high heat and cook for 20 minutes, or until
very tender. Drain well, then return to the saucepan. Add the garlic, olive oil,

milk and parsley and mash, using a potato masher, until smooth. Stir in the feta and season to taste with sea salt and freshly ground black pepper. Preheat the oven to 180°C (350°F/Gas 4).

• Heat the oil in a heavy-based saucepan over medium heat. Add the onion and cook, stirring occasionally, for 8 minutes, or until softened. Add the tomato, tomato paste, cardamom, pomegranate molasses, garlic and 125 ml (4 fl oz/½ cup) water. Cook for 10 minutes, stirring occasionally. Stir in the chickpeas and spinach and cook for 2–3 minutes, or until the spinach has wilted. Season to taste, then stir in the mint and coriander.

• Spoon the chickpea mixture into a 1.5 litre (52 fl oz/6 cup) baking dish, or divide among four 400 ml (14 fl oz) individual ovenproof dishes. Spoon the mashed potato over the top to cover.

• Bake for 20 minutes, or until the potato topping is lightly golden. Serve hot.

BAKED WHOLEMEAL CREPES WITH ASPARAGUS AND LEEK

preparation time 20 minutes plus 20 minutes standing
cooking time 1 hour 15 minutes
serves 4

16 asparagus spears, trimmed
130 g (4½ oz/1 cup) grated
   gruyère cheese
mixed leaf salad, to serve

CREPE BATTER
75 g (2½ oz/½ cup) wholemeal
   (whole-wheat) flour
75 g (2½ oz/½ cup) plain
   (all-purpose) flour
2 eggs, lightly beaten
375 ml (13 fl oz/1½ cups) milk

LEEK AND BASIL CREAM
40 g (1½ oz) butter
3 leeks, white part only, rinsed well
   and sliced
½ teaspoon freshly grated nutmeg
250 g (9 oz/1 cup) crème fraîche or
   sour cream
1 bunch (125 g/4½ oz) basil, leaves
   picked and finely chopped

● To make the crepe batter, sift the flours and a pinch of sea salt into a bowl, returning any wholemeal flour solids to the mixture. Make a well in the centre. Add the eggs and milk to the well then gradually whisk in the flour until the batter is smooth. Cover and leave to stand for 30 minutes.

● To make the leek and basil cream, melt the butter in a heavy-based saucepan over medium heat, then stir in the leek, nutmeg and 1 tablespoon water. Season to taste with sea salt and freshly ground black pepper, cover the pan, reduce the heat to low and cook for 40 minutes, or until the leek is very soft. Remove from the heat and allow to cool slightly, then stir in the crème fraîche and basil, and season to taste.

● While the leek is cooking, preheat the oven to 180°C (350°F/Gas 4). Heat a non-stick 15 cm (6 inch) crepe pan over medium heat. Spoon 80 ml (2½ fl oz/⅓ cup) of the crepe batter into the pan, swirling the pan so the mixture covers the base. Cook for 1–2 minutes, or until the edges of the batter start to lift from the pan. Carefully turn the crepe over and cook the other side for 1–2 minutes, then transfer to a plate. Cook the remaining batter to make eight crepes.

● Meanwhile, bring a saucepan of water to the boil. Add the asparagus and cook for 4–5 minutes, or until tender. Plunge into a bowl of iced water, then drain well and set aside.

● Place about 60 ml (2 fl oz/¼ cup) of the leek mixture and two asparagus spears down the centre of each crepe, then roll up to enclose the filling. Place the crepes in a single layer, seam side down, in a 15 x 30 cm (6 x 12 inch) baking dish. Sprinkle with the gruyère and bake for 10–12 minutes, or until the cheese has melted and the crepes are warmed through. Serve hot, with the mixed leaf salad.

STUFFED EGGPLANT ROLLS WITH SALSA VERDE

preparation time 25 minutes plus 20 minutes standing time
cooking time 55 minutes
serves 4

1 large eggplant (aubergine)
(about 675 g/1 lb 8 oz), trimmed
2 tablespoons sea salt
3 small (375 g/13 oz) washed
potatoes, peeled and chopped
185 ml (6 fl oz/¾ cup) olive oil
75 g (3 oz/¾ cup) grated parmesan
cheese
185 g (6½ oz/¾ cup) firm fresh
ricotta cheese
2 egg yolks
½ teaspoon freshly grated nutmeg

SALSA VERDE
2 large handfuls flat-leaf (Italian)
parsley
1 small handful mint
1 tablespoon capers, rinsed and
drained
3 anchovy fillets, drained
2 garlic cloves, chopped
1 tablespoon dijon mustard
2 tablespoons lemon juice
125 ml (4 fl oz/½ cup) good-quality
extra virgin olive oil

TOMATO SALAD
1 vine-ripened tomato
40 g (1½ oz/⅓ cup) hazelnuts,
roasted and chopped
1 small handful basil leaves

- Cut the eggplant lengthways into eight 5 mm (¼ inch) thick slices. Discard end slices. Layer slices in a colander, sprinkle each layer with salt and stand for 20 minutes. Rinse and pat dry with paper towels.

- Place the potatoes in saucepan and cover with cold water. Bring to the boil and cook for 7–10 minutes or until tender. Drain thoroughly, then mash with half the oil and half the parmesan. Transfer to a bowl to cool, then add ricotta, egg yolks and nutmeg and season to taste with sea salt and freshly ground black pepper.

- Heat a large heavy-based frying pan over medium heat. Brush the eggplant slices with the remaining oil and season with pepper. Fry eggplant in batches for 2–3 minutes on each side or until golden and tender. Transfer to a plate. Preheat oven to 180°C (350°F/Gas 4). Lay eggplant slices on a clean work surface and spoon 2 heaped tablespoons of the potato filling widthways across the centre of each slice. Roll to enclose filling and transfer to a lightly oiled baking dish, seam side down. Sprinkle rolls with remaining parmesan and bake for 25–35 minutes or until golden.

- For the salsa verde, place all ingredients except for the oil in the bowl of a food processor. Process until combined. Gradually add the oil with the motor running, process until smooth and season to taste.

- For the salad, bring a small saucepan of water to the boil. Cut a cross in the base of the tomato and boil for 2 minutes. Place in cold water. Peel away skin, cut into quarters, remove seeds and finely chop flesh. Combine with nuts and basil. Place 2 eggplant rolls on each serving plate, top with salsa verde and serve with salad.

Mains

VEGETARIAN 'MEATBALLS' IN NORTH AFRICAN-SPICED TOMATO SAUCE

preparation time 30 minutes plus 1 hour chillihg
cooking time 1 hour 20 minutes
serves 4–6

185 ml (6 fl oz/¾ cup) olive oil

2 brown onions, finely chopped

5 garlic cloves, crushed

50 g (2 oz/⅓ cup) currants

1 tablespoon cumin seeds, lightly toasted and coarsely crushed

500 g (1 lb 2 oz/6¼ cups) fresh breadcrumbs, made from day-old bread

200 g (7 oz/1⅓ cups) crumbled feta cheese

2 large handfuls mint leaves, chopped, plus extra, to garnish

2 large handfuls flat-leaf (Italian) parsley, chopped, plus extra, to garnish

4 eggs, lightly beaten

NORTH AFRICAN-SPICED TOMATO SAUCE

2 tablespoons olive oil

2 brown onions, finely chopped

1½ teaspoons paprika

½ teaspoon chilli powder, or to taste

½ teaspoon ground ginger

3 x 400 g (14 oz) tins chopped tomatoes

1 tablespoon finely chopped preserved lemon rind, or to taste, plus extra thin slices, to garnish

1 handful coriander (cilantro) leaves, finely chopped

- Heat 2 tablespoons of the olive oil in a non-stick frying pan over medium heat. Add the onion and cook, stirring, for 8 minutes, or until softened. Add the garlic, currants and cumin and cook for 1 minute.

- Line a baking tray with baking paper. Transfer the onion mixture to a large bowl and add the breadcrumbs, feta, mint, parsley and eggs. Season with sea salt and freshly ground black pepper, then mix well with your hands, adding a little milk if needed to bind the mixture together — the mixture should be firm and not sticky. Working with 2 tablespoons of the mixture at a time, form the mixture into balls. Place on the baking tray and refrigerate for 1 hour, or until firm.

- Meanwhile, make the North African-spiced tomato sauce. Heat the olive oil in a saucepan over medium heat. Add the onion and cook, stirring, for 8 minutes, or until softened. Add the spices and cook, stirring, for a further 1 minute, or until aromatic. Add the tomato and bring to the boil, then reduce the heat to low and simmer for 35–40 minutes, stirring occasionally, or until rich and thick. Stir in the preserved lemon and coriander and season to taste. Keep warm.

- Heat half the remaining oil in a frying pan over medium–high heat. Cook half the balls for 5–7 minutes, rolling them around in the pan to brown on all sides. Remove and drain on paper towels. Heat the remaining oil in the pan, cook the remaining balls.

- Divide the sauce among serving bowls. Top with the balls, garnish with the extra mint, parsley and preserved lemon, and serve.

Mains

BAKED RICOTTA-STUFFED EGGPLANT ROLLS

preparation time 35 minutes
cooking time 1 hour 55 minutes
serves 4

80 ml (2½ fl oz/⅓ cup) olive oil
1 brown onion, finely chopped
1 red capsicum (pepper), finely
   chopped
2 garlic cloves, crushed
2 tablespoons tomato paste
   (concentrated purée)
125 ml (4 fl oz/½ cup) dry white wine
2 x 400 g (14 oz) tins chopped
   tomatoes
1 teaspoon white sugar
2 eggplants (aubergines), about
    600 g (1 lb 5 oz), cut lengthways
    into 5 mm (¼ inch)-thick slices
2 tablespoons lemon juice
75 g (2½ oz/¾ cup) grated
   pecorino cheese
oregano, to garnish

RICOTTA STUFFING

400 g (14 oz/1⅔ cups) fresh
   ricotta cheese
2½ tablespoons oregano, chopped
1 teaspoon finely grated lemon rind
¾ teaspoon freshly grated nutmeg
75 g (3 oz/¾ cup) grated
   pecorino cheese
1 egg, lightly beaten
40 g (1½ oz/¼ cup) pine nuts, toasted
2 tablespoons finely chopped rinsed
   and drained capers

- Heat 1½ tablespoons of the olive oil in a heavy-based saucepan over medium–low heat. Add the onion and cook, stirring, for 8 minutes, or until softened. Add the capsicum and garlic and cook for 5 minutes.

- Stir in the tomato paste and cook for 30 seconds, then add the wine, tomato and sugar. Increase the heat to medium and bring to the boil, then reduce the heat to low and simmer gently, stirring occasionally, for 1 hour, or until the sauce has reduced and thickened. Season to taste with sea salt and freshly ground black pepper. Keep warm.

- Preheat the oven to 180°C (350°F/Gas 4). Heat a chargrill pan or barbecue hotplate to medium. Brush the eggplant slices with the remaining oil and season to taste. Chargrill in batches for 2 minutes on each side, or until golden and tender. Remove each batch to a plate and sprinkle with the lemon juice.

- To make the ricotta stuffing, combine all the ingredients in a bowl and season to taste.

- Lay the eggplant slices on a clean work surface. Divide the ricotta mixture among the wide ends of the eggplant slices, then roll each one into a firm roll. Place seam side down in a baking dish measuring about 28 x 19 x 6 cm (11 ¼ x 7½ x 2½ inches).

- Spoon the tomato sauce over the eggplant rolls and sprinkle with the pecorino. Bake for 35 minutes, or until the cheese is golden and bubbling. Garnish with oregano and serve.

GREEN VEGETABLE BAKE WITH PINE NUT AND PECORINO CRUMBLE

preparation time 30 minutes
cooking time 55 minutes
serves 4–6

155 g (5½ oz/1 cup) fresh shelled peas (about 375 g/13 oz unshelled peas)

1 large fennel bulb, trimmed, tough core removed, then cut into 2 cm (¾ inch) pieces

40 g (1½ oz) butter

2 bunches (600 g/1 lb 5 oz) English spinach, tough stems removed, leaves washed and dried

2 tablespoons olive oil

2 zucchini (courgettes), sliced into 2 cm (¾ inch)-thick rounds

1 teaspoon finely grated lemon rind

2 tablespoons lemon juice

¼ cup chopped dill

1 tablespoon chopped flat-leaf (Italian) parsley

250 g (9 oz/1 cup) ricotta cheese

150 ml (5 fl oz) thick (double/heavy) cream

CRUMBLE TOPPING

2 teaspoons fennel seeds

100 g (3½ oz/1 cup) grated pecorino cheese

40 g (1½ oz/¼ cup) pine nuts, coarsely chopped

80 g (3 oz/1 cup) fresh breadcrumbs

20 g (¾ oz) unsalted butter, chopped

● Preheat the oven to 190°C (375°F/Gas 5). Grease a 2 litre (70 fl oz/8 cup) baking dish.

● Bring a large saucepan of salted water to the boil. Add the peas and cook for 5 minutes, or until just tender. Using a slotted spoon, remove the peas to a large bowl. Add the fennel to the boiling water and cook for 5–6 minutes, or until just tender. Drain well, then pat dry with paper towels and set aside.

- Melt half the butter in a large non-stick frying pan over medium heat. Add the spinach and cook, stirring occasionally, for 2–3 minutes, or until the spinach has wilted and the liquid has almost evaporated. Drain very well, then transfer to the bowl with the peas.

- Return the frying pan to the heat and melt the remaining butter with 1 tablespoon of the olive oil. Add the blanched fennel and cook for 2 minutes on each side, or until golden brown; transfer to the bowl with the spinach. Heat the remaining oil in the pan, then add the zucchini and cook for 2 minutes on each side, or until golden; transfer to the bowl.

- Add the lemon rind, lemon juice, herbs, ricotta and cream to the sautéed vegetables and gently toss until well coated. Season to taste with sea salt and freshly ground black pepper. Spread the vegetable mixture in the baking dish.

- To make the crumble mixture, combine the fennel seeds, pecorino, pine nuts and breadcrumbs in a bowl. Sprinkle the crumble mixture over the vegetables and scatter the butter over the top.

- Bake for 20–25 minutes, or until bubbling and golden. Serve hot.

Mains

SPICY CAPSICUM AND TOMATO BAKE WITH EGG

preparation time 20 minutes
cooking time 55 minutes
serves 1

2 tablespoons olive oil

1 small red onion, cut into thin
    wedges

1 small red capsicum (pepper),
    seeded and thinly sliced

1 small yellow or orange capsicum
    (pepper), seeded and thinly sliced

1 garlic clove, crushed

1 scant teaspoon ground cumin

pinch of paprika

2 tomatoes, roughly chopped

2 teaspoons tomato paste
    (concentrated purée)

50 g (2 oz/⅓ cup) tinned cannellini
    beans, rinsed and drained

1½ tablespoons finely chopped
    flat-leaf (Italian) parsley

1 egg

toasted Turkish or pitta bread, to
    serve

- Preheat the oven to 180°C (350°F/Gas 4). Heat the oil in a frying pan over low heat. Add the onion, capsicum and garlic, and cook, stirring, for 15 minutes or until very soft.

- Add the cumin and paprika, and cook, stirring, for 1 minute or until fragrant. Add the tomato, tomato paste and 2 tablespoons water. Cook, stirring, for 15 minutes or until the tomato is very soft and a sauce has formed. Stir in the cannellini beans. Season to taste with sea salt and freshly ground black pepper, then stir in the parsley.

- Spoon the mixture into a 500 ml (17 fl oz/2 cup) capacity ovenproof ramekin (dariole mould). Make a well in the centre and break in the egg. Bake uncovered for 15–20 minutes or until the egg is just set. Serve immediately with the toasted Turkish or pitta bread on the side.

Mains

MUSHROOM AND SPINACH LASAGNE

preparation time 30 minutes
cooking time 30 minutes
serves 4

60 ml (2 fl oz/¼ cup) olive oil
60 g (2 oz) unsalted butter
300 g (10½ oz) large portobello or
field mushrooms, thinly sliced
200 g (7 oz) Swiss brown
mushrooms, thickly sliced
100 g (3½ oz) oyster mushrooms
150 g (5½ oz) shimeji or enoki
mushrooms, separated
200 g (7 oz) baby English spinach
leaves
3 garlic cloves, crushed

100 ml (3½ fl oz) verjuice
100 ml (3½ fl oz) vegetable stock
200 g (7 oz) crème fraîche or sour
cream
100 g (3½ oz) gorgonzola cheese,
crumbled
1 small handful marjoram, plus extra,
to garnish
4 fresh lasagne sheets (each about
10 x 14 cm/4 x 5½ inches)
30 g (1 oz/¼ cup) chopped roasted
hazelnuts

● Heat the oil and butter in a large non-stick frying pan over medium–high
heat. Reserving the enoki mushrooms, sauté all the other mushrooms for
5 minutes, or until browned and softened. Add the enoki mushrooms, baby
spinach and garlic and cook for 1 minute. Stir in the verjuice and stock and
bring to the boil, then reduce the heat to low. Stir in the crème fraîche,
gorgonzola and marjoram. Simmer over medium heat for 1 minute, or until
reduced to a light sauce consistency. Season to taste with sea salt and freshly
ground black pepper.

● Bring two large saucepans of salted water to the boil. Cut each sheet of
lasagne widthways into three even-sized squares or rectangles. Cook the pasta
in the boiling water for 3–4 minutes, or until al dente. Drain.

● Place a lasagne sheet portion on each serving plate. Spoon one-third of the spinach and mushrooms over the top. Add another lasagne sheet portion to each and top with half of the remaining spinach and mushrooms. Arrange the remaining pasta over the top and spoon over the remaining spinach and mushrooms. Sprinkle with the hazelnuts, then garnish with the extra marjoram.

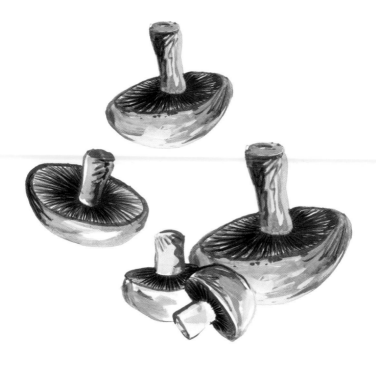

ROAST PUMPKIN AND MOZZARELLA LASAGNE

preparation time 30 minutes
cooking time 1 hour 30 minutes
serves 4–6

1 kg (2 lb 4 oz) pumpkin (winter squash), peeled and cut into slices 1 cm (½ inch) thick
olive oil
250 g (9 oz) dried lasange sheets
225 g (8 oz) mozzarella cheese, grated

TOMATO, BASIL AND CINNAMON SAUCE
80 ml (2½ fl oz/⅓ cup) extra virgin olive oil
3 onions, finely chopped
3 garlic cloves, finely chopped
2 tablespoons tomato paste (concentrated purée)
330 ml (11 fl oz/1⅓ cups) red wine
5 x 400 g (14 oz) tins chopped tomatoes
3 teaspoons caster (superfine) sugar
1½ tablespoons balsamic vinegar
1½ cinnamon sticks
1 small handful basil leaves, torn

- Preheat the oven to 180°C (350°F/Gas 4). Lightly oil a large roasting tin. To make the tomato, basil and cinnamon sauce, heat the olive oil in a large saucepan over medium heat. Add the onion and garlic and sauté for 8 minutes, or until the onion is soft. Add the tomato paste and cook, stirring, for 2 minutes, then add the wine and boil for 2–3 minutes, or until slightly reduced. Stir in the tomatoes, sugar, vinegar and cinnamon sticks. Bring the mixture to a simmer, then reduce the heat to low and cook for 25 minutes. Discard the cinnamon sticks and season to taste with sea salt and freshly ground black pepper. Stir in the basil.

- Meanwhile, lay the pumpkin slices in overlapping layers in the tin, then drizzle with olive oil. Bake for 20 minutes, or until tender.

- Grease a 30 x 20 cm (12 x 8 inch) baking dish, then spread about one-quarter of the tomato sauce over the base. Place a single layer of lasagne sheets over the sauce. Spread half the pumpkin over in a single layer and spread with about another one-quarter of the sauce.

- Scatter one-third of the cheese over the sauce. Add another layer of lasagne sheets, then the remaining pumpkin, another one-quarter of the sauce and another one-third of the mozzarella. Top with a final layer of lasagne sheets, spread the remaining tomato sauce over and sprinkle with the remaining mozzarella; you may not need to use all the sauce.

- Cover with oiled foil and bake for 30 minutes. Remove the foil and bake for another 20 minutes, or until the cheese is golden and bubbling.

LINGUINE SALAD WITH RADICCHIO, OLIVES AND BASIL

preparation time 20 minutes
cooking time 15 minutes
serves 4–6

400 g (14 oz) linguine
60 ml (2 fl oz/¼ cup) extra virgin olive oil, plus extra, to serve
2 small red onions, peeled and thinly sliced
95 g (3 oz/½ cup) chopped pitted kalamata olives
2 teaspoons finely grated lemon rind
60 ml (2 fl oz/¼ cup) lemon juice
2 garlic cloves, crushed

80 g (3 oz/1 cup) coarse breadcrumbs, made from day-old bread
2 tablespoons flat-leaf (Italian) parsley, coarsely chopped
1 large handful basil, thinly sliced, reserving 12 leaves to garnish
2 small or ½ large head of radicchio, leaves trimmed and thinly sliced
purchased tapenade, to serve (optional)

- Cook the linguine in a large saucepan of salted, boiling water according to packet instructions or until al dente. Drain well in a colander, then combine in a large bowl with 1 tablespoon of the olive oil. Set aside.

- Heat 1 tablespoon of the olive oil in a large frying pan over medium heat. Add the onion and cook, stirring, for 2–3 minutes or until starting to soften, then add the olives, lemon rind and juice and stir until well combined. Add to the pasta in the bowl.

- Wipe the frying pan clean and heat the remaining olive oil over medium–high heat. Add the garlic and cook for 30 seconds or until golden. Add the breadcrumbs and cook, stirring often, for 3 minutes or until crumbs are golden. Remove from the heat and stir in the chopped parsley.

• Add the basil and radicchio to the pasta mixture in the bowl, then season well with sea salt and freshly ground black pepper. Toss to combine well. Divide the salad among bowls. Drizzle with the extra virgin olive oil, sprinkle with garlic crumbs and garnish with basil leaves. Serve immediately with a little tapenade spooned over, if using.

PENNE WITH PESTO, BOCCONCINI AND CHERRY TOMATOES

preparation time 10 minutes
cooking time 20 minutes
serves 4–6

500 g (1 lb 2 oz) penne pasta
1 tablespoon extra virgin olive oil
250 g (9 oz) cherry tomatoes, halved
190 g (7 oz) jar pesto
2 large handfuls baby English spinach
    leaves
1 small handful basil, roughly
    chopped

60 ml (2 fl oz/¼ cup) cream
25 g (1 oz/¼ cup) grated parmesan
    cheese, plus extra, to serve
1 garlic clove, crushed
2 tablespoons pine nuts
1 teaspoon finely grated lemon rind
180 g (6 oz) bocconcini (fresh baby
    mozzarella cheese), torn

● Bring a large saucepan of salted water to the boil. Add the pasta and cook according to the packet instructions, until al dente. Drain well and set aside.

● Place the saucepan back over medium heat. Add the olive oil and tomatoes and cook for 2–3 minutes, or until the tomatoes have softened slightly. Add the pesto, drained pasta, spinach leaves, basil, cream and parmesan. Cook for 3–5 minutes, or until heated through, stirring to combine well.

● Remove from the heat, then add the garlic, pine nuts, lemon rind and bocconcini, tossing to combine well.

● Season to taste with sea salt and freshly ground black pepper and divide among warm bowls. Sprinkle with extra parmesan and serve.

CREAMY RICOTTA RAVIOLI WITH SILVERBEET, NUTMEG AND LEMON

preparation time 10 minutes
cooking time 25 minutes
serves 4

500 g (1 lb 2 oz) fresh ricotta ravioli or ricotta tortellini
2½ tablespoons olive oil
1 small onion, finely chopped
1 garlic clove, crushed
400 g (14 oz/½ bunch) silverbeet (Swiss chard), stems removed, leaves washed, dried and thinly sliced

a large pinch of freshly grated nutmeg
250 ml (9 fl oz/1 cup) cream
2 tablespoons capers, rinsed and drained
2 tablespoons lemon juice
1 tomato, seeded and finely chopped
35 g (1 oz/⅓ cup) grated parmesan cheese

Mains

- Bring a large saucepan of salted water to the boil. Add the pasta and cook according to the packet instructions until al dente. Drain the pasta, reserving the pan, and set the pasta aside in a bowl. Gently toss ½ tablespoon of the olive oil through the pasta to stop it sticking together.

- Heat the remaining oil in the saucepan, add the onion and sauté over medium heat for 5 minutes, or until softened. Add the garlic, silverbeet and nutmeg and cook for a further 3−4 minutes, or until the silverbeet has wilted.

- Pour in the cream, bring to the boil, then reduce the heat to a simmer and cook for 3−4 minutes, or until the liquid has reduced by half. Return the ravioli to the pan, add the capers and lemon juice and gently toss to combine well.

- Season to taste with sea salt and freshly ground black pepper, scatter the chopped tomato and grated parmesan over and serve.

LINGUINE WITH GREEN BEANS, POTATO AND MINT AND ALMOND PESTO

preparation time 20 minutes
cooking time 20 minutes
serves 4

3 desiree or other all-purpose
    potatoes (about 400 g/14 oz),
    diced
200 g (7 oz) green beans, trimmed
    and cut into short lengths
400 g (14 oz) linguine
green salad, to serve

MINT AND ALMOND PESTO
60 g (2 oz/⅓ cup) blanched almonds
1 garlic clove, sliced
25 g (1 oz/1¼ cups) mint leaves,
    lightly packed
1 small handful flat-leaf (Italian)
    parsley
125 ml (4 fl oz/½ cup) extra virgin
    olive oil
50 g (2 oz/½ cup) grated pecorino
    cheese, plus extra, to serve

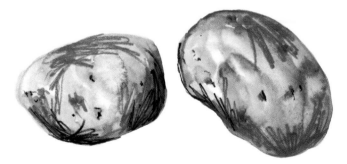

• Preheat the oven to 180°C (350°F/Gas 4). To make the mint and almond pesto, spread the almonds on a baking tray and toast in the oven for 4–5 minutes, or until lightly toasted. Allow to cool, then transfer to a food processor with the garlic and blend until finely chopped. Add the mint, parsley and olive oil, and blend until well combined. Add the pecorino and pulse until just combined. Season to taste with sea salt and freshly ground black pepper, and set aside.

• Bring a large saucepan of salted water to the boil. Add the potato and cook for 10 minutes, then add the beans and cook for a further 3 minutes, or until the vegetables are tender. Drain well.

• Meanwhile, cook the pasta in another saucepan of boiling salted water until al dente, following the packet instructions. Drain well, reserving 2 tablespoons of the cooking water.

• Return the hot pasta to the saucepan with the reserved cooking water. Add the potato, beans and pesto, and toss together until well combined. Divide among serving bowls. Serve scattered with extra grated pecorino, with a green salad on the side.

FETTUCCINE WITH ROAST FENNEL, SAFFRON, OLIVES AND BREADCRUMBS

preparation time 15 minutes plus 30 minutes soaking
cooking time 45 minutes
serves 4

a large pinch of saffron threads
60 ml (2 fl oz/¼ cup) white wine
4 fennel bulbs, trimmed, tough cores
  removed, then thinly sliced
2 red onions, halved and thinly sliced
4 garlic cloves, finely chopped
125 ml (4 fl oz/½ cup) olive oil
80 g (3 oz) day-old sourdough bread,
  crusts removed
500 g (1 lb 2 oz) fresh fettuccine

80 g (3 oz/½ cup) pitted kalamata
  olives, sliced
40 g (1½ oz/¼ cup) toasted pine nuts
1½ tablespoons chopped oregano
3 tablespoons chopped flat-leaf
  (Italian) parsley
1 small handful baby rocket (arugula)
shaved parmesan cheese, to serve
  (optional)

• Preheat the oven to 180°C (350°F/Gas 4). Put the saffron in a small bowl,
pour in the wine and leave to soak for 30 minutes.

• Place the fennel, onion and garlic in a baking dish. Drizzle with 80 ml
(2½ fl oz/⅓ cup) of the olive oil and toss to coat. Bake for 45 minutes, or until
the fennel is golden and tender.

• Reduce the oven temperature to 120°C (235°F/Gas ½). Add the saffron and
wine to the fennel and onion mixture, then return to the oven to keep warm.

• Meanwhile, put the bread in a food processor and pulse until coarse crumbs
form. Heat the remaining olive oil in a heavy-based frying pan, add the
breadcrumbs and stir over medium–low heat for 5–6 minutes, or until crisp
and golden. Drain on paper towels and set aside.

● Bring a large saucepan of salted water to the boil. Add the fettuccine and cook for 3–4 minutes, or until al dente. Drain well, then return to the pan.

● Add the fennel mixture to the saucepan with the olives, pine nuts, herbs, rocket and breadcrumbs. Toss well to combine.

● Divide the pasta among serving bowls. Serve scattered with parmesan shavings if desired.

Mains

SPAGHETTI WITH LEEK, ORANGE, BASIL AND SUN-DRIED TOMATOES

preparation time 20 minutes
cooking time 20 minutes
serves 4???

500 g (1 lb 2 oz) spaghetti
30 g (1 oz) unsalted butter
4 leeks, white part only, rinsed well
   and thinly sliced
2 garlic cloves, crushed
300 ml (10½ fl oz) cream
2½ teaspoons finely grated orange
   rind

80 ml (2½ fl oz/⅓ cup) orange juice
1 small handful basil, chopped
80 g (3 oz/½ cup) thinly sliced
   semi-dried (sun-blushed) tomatoes
50 g (2 oz/½ cup) shaved parmesan
   cheese

• Add the spaghetti to a large saucepan of rapidly boiling salted water and cook according to the packet instructions until al dente, about 10 minutes. Drain well.

• Meanwhile, melt the butter in a large frying pan. Once the butter has melted, add the leek, season with sea salt and freshly ground black pepper and sauté gently over medium–low heat for about 5 minutes, or until softened and light golden brown.

• Add the garlic to the frying pan and cook for 2 minutes, then add the cream, orange rind and orange juice and simmer for 3–5 minutes.

• Add the drained pasta, basil and sun-dried tomatoes to the frying pan, then toss well to coat the pasta with the sauce.

• Divide the pasta among serving bowls, scatter with the parmesan and serve.

Note *Any leftover pasta can be refrigerated in an airtight container for up to 3 days, but is not suitable for freezing.*

Mains

RICOTTA GNOCCHI WITH TOMATO, BASIL AND CINNAMON SAUCE

preparation time 45 minutes
cooking time 45 minutes
serves 4

750 g (1 lb 10 oz) firm fresh ricotta
225 g (8 oz/1½ cups) plain
   (all-purpose) flour, sifted,
   plus extra, for dusting
3 eggs
1 teaspoon freshly grated nutmeg
shredded or grated parmesan cheese,
   to serve

TOMATO, BASIL AND CINNAMON SAUCE

80 ml (2½ fl oz/⅓ cup) extra virgin
   olive oil
3 onions, finely chopped
3 garlic cloves, finely chopped
2 tablespoons tomato paste
   (concentrated purée)
330 ml (11 fl oz/1⅓ cups) red wine
5 x 400 g (14 oz) tins chopped
   tomatoes
3 teaspoons caster (superfine) sugar
1½ tablespoons balsamic vinegar
1½ cinnamon sticks
1 small handful basil leaves, torn

plain
flour

• To make the tomato, basil and cinnamon sauce, heat the olive oil in a large saucepan over medium heat. Add the onion and garlic and sauté for 8 minutes, or until the onion is soft. Add the tomato paste and cook, stirring, for 2 minutes, then add the wine and boil for 2–3 minutes, or until slightly reduced. Stir in the tomatoes, sugar, vinegar and cinnamon sticks. Bring the mixture to a simmer, then reduce the heat to low and cook for 25 minutes. Discard the cinnamon sticks and season to taste with sea salt and freshly ground black pepper. Just before serving, stir in the basil.

• Meanwhile, combine the ricotta in a large bowl with the flour, eggs and nutmeg. Season to taste, then mix together well.

• Dust a work surface with flour. Divide the ricotta mixture into six portions. Using your hands, roll each portion into a rope about 2 cm (¾ inch) thick, then cut each one into 3 cm (1¼ inch) lengths.

Mains

• Bring a large saucepan of salted water to the boil. Add the gnocchi in batches and cook for 3–4 minutes, or until they rise to the surface and are cooked through. Remove using a slotted spoon and keep warm.

• Divide the gnocchi among serving bowls, then spoon some of the sauce over. Scatter with parmesan and serve.

Note *This recipe makes a generous quantity of sauce. Keep any leftover sauce in an airtight container in the refrigerator for up to 2 days and use with another pasta dish.*

ROASTED PUMPKIN GNOCCHI WITH THREE-CHEESE SAUCE

preparation time 30 minutes
cooking time 45 minutes
serves 4

1 kg (2 lb 4 oz) butternut pumpkin
   (squash), peeled and cut into
   1 cm (½ inch)-thick slices
1 tablespoon olive oil
350 g (12 oz/1⅓ cups) firm fresh
   ricotta cheese
1 egg yolk
110 g (4 oz/1 cup) finely grated
   parmesan cheese
100 g (3½ oz/⅔ cup) plain
   (all-purpose) flour, plus extra, for
   dusting
40 g (1½ oz) butter
50 g (2 oz/½ cup) toasted
   walnuts, chopped
finely grated rind of 1 lemon
thyme sprigs, to garnish

THREE-CHEESE SAUCE
60 g (2 oz/¼ cup) firm ricotta cheese
60 g (2 oz/¼ cup) mascarpone cheese
40 g (1½ oz/⅓ cup) blue cheese,
   crumbled
2½ tablespoons milk

• Preheat the oven to 200°C (400°F/Gas 6). Line two baking trays with baking paper.

• Toss the pumpkin in the olive oil and spread on the baking trays. Sprinkle with sea salt and roast for 20 minutes. Then turn each piece over and roast for a further 20 minutes, or until most of the excess moisture has evaporated and the pumpkin is tender. Transfer to a bowl and mash until smooth, then set aside to cool completely.

- Meanwhile, to make the three-cheese sauce, place all the ingredients in a food processor and pulse until well combined. Transfer to a saucepan and set aside.

- Bring a large saucepan of salted water to the boil. Reduce the heat to a simmer, then cover the pan to stop the water evaporating.

- Press the ricotta through a sieve, into the cooled pumpkin. Add the egg yolk and 25 g (1 oz/¼ cup) of the parmesan and mix until thoroughly combined. Season to taste with sea salt and freshly ground black pepper. Add the flour and mix until just combined; the mixture will be soft. Divide the mixture into four portions. Place one portion on a very lightly floured surface. Using your hands, roll it into a log 2 cm (¾ inch) in diameter, adding a little more flour if it sticks to the surface. Cut into 3 cm (1¼ inch)-long pieces and set aside. Repeat with the remaining mixture.

- Melt the butter in a large saucepan over medium–low heat. Add half the gnocchi to the simmering pan of water. As soon as the gnocchi rise to the surface (after about 1 minute), remove them with a slotted spoon and gently toss to coat in the melted butter. Repeat with the remaining gnocchi.

- Meanwhile, heat the three-cheese sauce over medium–low heat, stirring occasionally, until hot but not simmering. Divide the gnocchi among four warmed plates or shallow bowls. Spoon the sauce over, then scatter with the walnuts and lemon rind. Garnish with thyme and serve.

Mains

BEETROOT, RED WINE AND BORLOTTI BEAN RISOTTO

preparation time 30 minutes
cooking time 1 hour 40 minutes
serves 4–6

5 small beetroot (beets), about 650 g
   (1 lb 7 oz), with stems and leaves
2 tablespoons olive oil
25 g (1 oz) butter
1 large brown onion
2 garlic cloves, finely chopped
2 rosemary sprigs
1.25 litres (44 fl oz/5 cups) vegetable
   stock

330 g (11½ oz/1½ cups) arborio rice
250 ml (9 fl oz/1 cup) red wine
50 g (2 oz/⅓ cup) currants
400 g (14 oz/2 cups) tinned borlotti
   (cranberry) beans, rinsed and
   drained
100 g (3½ oz/1 cup) finely grated
   parmesan cheese

● Trim the stems from the beetroot, leaving about 1 cm (½ inch) attached and reserving the stems and leaves. Place the beetroot in a small saucepan, cover with water, then bring to a simmer over medium heat. Cook for 50–60 minutes, or until nearly tender when pierced with a skewer, then drain well and allow to cool slightly. Using your hands, peel off the skins, then chop the beetroot and set aside.

● Heat the olive oil and butter in a large saucepan over medium heat. Add the onion and garlic and cook, stirring, for 5 minutes, or until the onion is starting to soften. Add the beetroot and rosemary. Cover and cook, stirring often, for 15 minutes, or until the beetroot is tender. Chop the reserved beetroot stems and leaves and add them to the pan.

● Meanwhile, bring the stock to a simmer in a saucepan, then cover, reduce heat and keep at a simmer.

- Add the rice to the beetroot mixture and cook, stirring, for 2–3 minutes, or until the rice is heated through. Add the wine and stir until it has been absorbed. Add 250 ml (9 fl oz/1 cup) of the hot stock, then cook, stirring, until the stock has been absorbed. Add another 250 ml (9 fl oz/1 cup) of stock and stir until the stock has been absorbed. Continue adding the stock and stirring the rice until the stock has been almost all absorbed and the rice is just tender — the mixture should be creamy.

- Stir in the currants and borlotti beans and cook for 2 minutes, or until heated through.

- Divide the risotto among serving bowls, scatter with the parmesan and serve.

MUSHROOM, RED WINE AND BARLEY RISOTTO

preparation time 20 minutes
cooking time 1 hour 30 minutes
serves 6

1 litre (35 fl oz/4 cups) vegetable
   stock
40 g (1½ oz) butter
500 g (1 lb 2 oz) Swiss brown
   mushrooms, quartered
2 tablespoons olive oil
1 onion, finely chopped
2 garlic cloves, crushed
2 tablespoons finely chopped

rosemary
300 g (10½ oz/1⅓ cups) pearl barley
125 ml (4 fl oz/½ cup) red wine
2 tablespoons torn parsley leaves
1 tablespoon crème fraiche or
   sour cream
shaved pecorino cheese, to serve

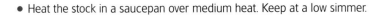

● Heat the stock in a saucepan over medium heat. Keep at a low simmer.

● Meanwhile, melt the butter in a large frying pan over medium–high heat. Add the mushrooms and sauté for 5–6 minutes, or until softened and light golden. Remove to a plate.

● Heat the olive oil in the saucepan over medium heat. Add the onion and sauté for 5–6 minutes, or until the onion has softened. Add the garlic and rosemary and cook for 1–2 minutes. Add the barley and stir until well coated.

● Pour in the wine and continue to stir until the liquid is almost absorbed.

When the wine has been absorbed, add a ladle of hot stock to the barley and continue to stir slowly until the stock has been absorbed.

● Add the remaining stock, then cover and simmer for 1 hour, or until the barley is tender.

● Stir in the mushrooms with any juices, along with the parsley and crème fraiche. Cook, uncovered, for 10 minutes. Season to taste with sea salt and freshly ground black pepper.

● Divide the risotto among serving bowls. Scatter with shaved pecorino cheese and serve.

Note *Any leftover risotto can be refrigerated in an airtight container for up to 2 days.*

SOFT CHEESE AND WALNUT POLENTA WITH MUSHROOMS

preparation time 15 minutes
cooking time 20 minutes
serves 1

2 large field mushrooms, trimmed
  and peeled
1 tablespoon olive oil
310 ml (11 fl oz/1¼ cups)
  vegetable stock
60 ml (2 fl oz/¼ cup) milk
45 g (2 oz/¼ cup) instant polenta

15 g (½ oz) butter
30 g (1 oz/¼ cup) walnut pieces,
  toasted and chopped
2 tablespoons shaved pecorino
  cheese
snipped chives, to serve

● Heat a chargrill pan or small, heavy-based frying pan over medium heat. Brush the mushrooms with the oil and cook, cap side down, for 3 minutes, then turn and cook for 3–4 minutes or until the mushrooms are tender. Remove from the heat, cover and set aside.

● Combine the stock and milk in a small saucepan and bring to the boil over medium heat. Stirring constantly, gradually add the polenta in a steady stream, then cook, whisking constantly, until the mixture boils and thickens. Reduce the heat to low and cook, stirring often, for 5–6 minutes or until the mixture is very thick. Remove from the heat and add the butter and most of the walnuts and pecorino, reserving some for garnish. Mix well to combine.

● To serve, spoon the polenta into a shallow bowl, top with the mushrooms, garnish with the remaining walnuts and pecorino, sprinkle with the chives and serve immediately.

Mains

PUY LENTILS WITH CHESTNUTS AND SPINACH ON SOFT POLENTA

preparation time 25 minutes plus 2 hours chilling

cooking time 1 hour 10 minutes

serves 4

200 g (7 oz) frozen peeled chestnuts,
  or 400 g (14 oz) fresh chestnuts,
  peeled

2 tablespoons olive oil

1 small fennel bulb, trimmed, tough
  cores removed, then thinly sliced

1 celery stalk, thinly sliced

2 garlic cloves

2 tablespoons thyme, chopped,
  plus extra, to garnish

1 tablespoon tomato paste
  (concentrated purée)

375 g (13 oz/2 cups) puy lentils

1 bay leaf

2 vine-ripened tomatoes, chopped

185 ml (6 fl oz/¾ cup) white wine

750 ml (26 fl oz/3 cups) vegetable
  stock

80 g (3 oz/1¾ cups) baby English
  spinach leaves

1 small handful flat-leaf (Italian)
  parsley, coarsely chopped

POLENTA

500 ml (17 fl oz/2 cups) vegetable
  stock

500 ml (17 fl oz/2 cups) milk

½ teaspoon sea salt

175 g (6 oz) polenta

100 g (3½ oz) taleggio cheese,
  chopped

60 ml (2 fl oz/¼ cup) cream

- Cook the chestnuts in a saucepan of salted boiling water for 4 minutes. Drain well, then cut into quarters and set aside.

- Heat the olive oil in a heavy-based saucepan over medium–low heat. Add the fennel, celery, garlic and thyme. Cook, stirring, for 8–10 minutes, or until the vegetables have softened and caramelised slightly. Stir in the tomato paste and cook for 30 seconds.

- Stir in the lentils, bay leaf and tomato, then pour in the wine and stock. Increase the heat to medium and bring to the boil, then reduce the heat to low, cover and simmer for 30 minutes.

- Add the chestnuts, then cover and cook for a further 20 minutes, or until the lentils are tender. Stir in the baby spinach and parsley and cook for 2–3 minutes, or until the spinach has wilted. Remove from the heat, season to taste with sea salt and freshly ground black pepper, and keep warm.

- While the lentils are simmering, make the polenta. Bring the stock and milk to the boil in a heavy-based saucepan over high heat. Stir in the salt and reduce the heat to medium–low. Gradually add the polenta in a thin steady stream, whisking constantly until smooth. Cook, stirring constantly, for 15 minutes, or until the polenta is very thick and pulls away from the side of the pan. Remove from the heat and stir in the taleggio and cream until combined. Season to taste.

- Divide the polenta among serving bowls and spoon the lentil mixture over. Garnish with extra thyme and serve.

Mains

CHICKPEA BURGERS

preparation time 25 minutes
cooking time 35 minutes
serves 6

80 ml (2½ fl oz/⅓ cup) olive oil
6 x 15 cm (6 inch) wholemeal
    (whole-wheat) pitta breads
3 tomatoes, sliced
2 avocados, sliced
1 baby cos (romaine) lettuce, leaves
    washed and dried
Greek yoghurt, to serve
mint leaves, to serve

CHICKPEA PATTIES
2 large desiree potatoes, about 550 g
    (1 lb 4 oz) in total, peeled and
    chopped into 3 cm (1¼ inch)
    chunks
2 x 400 g (14 oz) tins chickpeas,
    rinsed and drained
1 tablespoon tahini
4 garlic cloves, finely chopped
6 spring onions (scallions), thinly
    sliced
1 long red chilli, finely chopped
1 carrot, grated
1 teaspoon ground cumin
1 teaspoon ground coriander

● To make the chickpea patties, cook the potatoes in a saucepan of boiling
salted water for 20–25 minutes, or until tender. Drain and allow to cool, then
mash and set aside.

● Place the chickpeas in a food processor and blend until roughly chopped.
Transfer to a large bowl and add the mashed potato, tahini, garlic, spring onion,
chilli, carrot, cumin and coriander. Season with sea salt and freshly ground
black pepper and mix well. Divide the mixture into 12 even portions, then shape
into patties.

● Heat half the olive oil in a large heavy-based frying pan over medium heat. Add half the patties and cook for 3 minutes each side, or until golden, taking care as you turn them as the patties are quite fragile. Remove and drain on kitchen paper, then repeat with the remaining oil and patties.

● To assemble the burgers, cut the pitta breads horizontally to open them up slightly. Divide the patties, tomato, avocado and lettuce among the pitta breads. Spoon in some yoghurt, top with mint leaves and serve.

Mains

TOFU BURGERS WITH SWEET CHILLI MAYONNAISE

preparation time 20 minutes plus 30 minutes chilling
cooking time 10 minutes
serves 6

2 tablespoons vegetable oil
6 burger buns, split in half, toasted
1 Lebanese (short) cucumber, thinly
    sliced lengthways
100 g (3½ oz) bean sprouts, tails
    trimmed
½ red capsicum (pepper), very thinly
    sliced
sweet chilli sauce, to serve

TOFU PATTIES

600 g (1 lb 5 oz) firm tofu, drained
    well
1 carrot, coarsely grated
3 garlic cloves, crushed
3 cm (1¼ inch) piece of fresh ginger,
    peeled and finely grated
2 tablespoons white miso paste
1 tablespoon soy sauce
1 egg, lightly beaten
2 tablespoons finely chopped
    coriander (cilantro) leaves
80 g (3 oz/½ cup) sesame seeds

SWEET CHILLI MAYONNAISE

125 g (4½ oz/½ cup) whole-egg
    mayonnaise
60 ml (2 fl oz/¼ cup) sweet chilli
    sauce

- To make the tofu patties, coarsely grate the tofu into a large bowl. Using your hands, squeeze out and discard any excess liquid from the tofu. Add the remaining patty ingredients, except the sesame seeds, to the tofu and mix together well until the mixture holds its shape. Shape into six patties about 7.5 cm (3 inches) in diameter. Spread the sesame seeds on a plate and coat each patty with them, pressing them on firmly. Refrigerate the patties for 30 minutes, or until firm.

- Meanwhile, to make the sweet chilli mayonnaise, place the ingredients in a small bowl and mix until well combined. Cover and refrigerate until serving time.

- Heat the oil in a large non-stick frying pan over medium heat. Add the patties and cook for 3 minutes on each side, or until golden and heated through.

- Place the burger bun bases on serving plates. Top with the patties, then add the cucumber, bean sprouts and capsicum. Add a dollop of the sweet chilli mayonnaise and a little sweet chilli sauce, top with the burger lids and serve.

Mains

TOFU STEAK WITH FRIED EGGPLANT, DAIKON AND RED MISO DRESSING

preparation time 10 minutes plus 30 minutes standing
cooking time 20 minutes
serves 4

2 small eggplants (aubergines),
    about 700 g (1 lb 9 oz), each cut
    into 8 wedges
250 ml (9 fl oz/1 cup) vegetable oil
rice flour, for dusting
freshly ground white pepper, for
    seasoning
600 g (1 lb 5 oz) firm tofu, drained
    and cut into 1 cm (½ inch)-thick
    slices
90 g (3 oz/1 cup) finely grated daikon
mixed baby salad greens, to serve

RED MISO DRESSING
2 teaspoons instant dashi powder
1 tablespoon red miso paste
1 tablespoon tamari
1½ tablespoons mirin
1 teaspoon sugar

● Place the eggplant in a colander and sprinkle with sea salt. Leave to stand for 30 minutes, then rinse well and pat dry using paper towels.

● Preheat the oven to 120°C (235°F/Gas ½). Heat 80 ml (2½ fl oz/⅓ cup) of the oil in a non-stick frying pan over medium–high heat. Add half the eggplant and cook for 2 minutes on each side, or until golden. Remove and drain on paper towels on a baking tray. Fry the remaining eggplant, adding more oil to the pan as necessary. Drain on paper towels, then transfer the baking tray to the oven to keep warm.

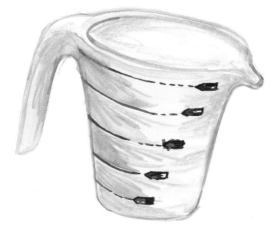

● Season some rice flour with freshly ground white pepper. Pat the tofu slices dry with paper towels, then lightly coat in the rice flour, dusting off the excess. Heat the remaining oil in the frying pan over medium–high heat. Cook the tofu for 1–2 minutes on each side, or until golden. Remove from the pan and drain on paper towels.

● Meanwhile, make the red miso dressing. Bring 200 ml (7 fl oz) water to a simmer in a saucepan. Add the dressing ingredients and stir to dissolve the sugar — do not allow to boil.

● Divide the tofu among shallow serving bowls. Top with the eggplant wedges and spoon the dressing over. Scatter with the daikon, garnish with salad greens and serve.

SALT AND PEPPER TOFU WITH SNOW PEAS

preparation time 25 minutes
cooking time 15 minutes
serves 4

2 teaspoons freshly ground
   sichuan peppercorns
1 teaspoon freshly ground
   white pepper
2 tablespoons sea salt
75 g (2½ oz/½ cup) plain
   (all-purpose) flour
600 g (1 lb 5 oz) firm silken tofu,
   drained and cut into 8 squares

350 g (12 oz) snow peas
   (mangetout), trimmed
1 litre (35 fl oz/4 cups) vegetable oil
5 garlic cloves, thinly sliced
2 long red chillies, thinly sliced on the
   diagonal
8 red Asian shallots, thinly sliced on
   the diagonal
steamed rice, to serve
lemon wedges, to serve
soy sauce, to serve

- Place the peppercorns, salt and flour in a bowl and mix well. Working in batches, gently coat the tofu with the flour mixture, shaking off the excess. Set aside on a plate.

- Bring a saucepan of lightly salted water to the boil over medium–high heat. Blanch the snow peas for 30 seconds, drain well, then transfer to a plate and keep warm.

- Heat the oil in a saucepan over medium–high heat to 180°C (350°F). The oil is ready when a cube of bread dropped into the oil turns golden in 15 seconds.

• Add half the tofu to the oil and deep-fry for 1–2 minutes, or until golden and crisp. Remove with a slotted spoon and drain on paper towels. Repeat with the remaining tofu.

• Add the garlic, chilli and shallot to the oil and cook for 1 minute. Remove using a slotted spoon and drain on paper towels.

• Divide the steamed rice among serving bowls. Top with the tofu and snow peas, then garnish with the fried garlic, chilli and shallot. Serve with lemon wedges and soy sauce.

Mains

177

TOFU, CASHEW AND NOODLE STIR-FRY

preparation time 15 minutes
cooking time 10
serves 4

300 g (10½ oz) fresh hokkien (egg) noodles or fresh rice noodles
1 teaspoon sesame oil
2 tablespoons soy sauce
60 ml (2 fl oz/¼ cup) vegetarian oyster sauce (see Note)
2 tablespoons vegetable oil
1 onion, thinly sliced
2 garlic cloves, thinly sliced
1 tablespoon grated fresh ginger
200 g (7 oz/1 bunch) broccolini, stems and heads halved lengthways, then cut into 5 cm (2 inch) lengths

300 g (10½ oz/1 bunch) bok choy (pak choy), trimmed and cut into 5 cm (2 inch) lengths
150 g (5½ oz) firm tofu, cut into 2 cm (¾ inch) chunks
100 g (3½ oz) snow peas (mangetout), cut in half on the diagonal
50 g (2 oz/⅓ cup) roasted cashew nuts

- Put the noodles in a large heatproof bowl and pour in enough boiling water to cover. Leave to stand for 2–3 minutes, or until softened, then drain well.

- In a small bowl, mix together the sesame oil, soy sauce, oyster sauce and 60 ml (2 fl oz/¼ cup) water. Set aside.

- Heat the vegetable oil in a wok over high heat. Stir-fry the onion and garlic for 1 minute, then add the ginger, broccolini and bok choy and stir-fry for another minute.

- Add the drained noodles, tofu and snow peas and stir-fry for 1–2 minutes, then add the soy sauce mixture and stir-fry for another 2–3 minutes, or until the liquid boils and the vegetables are tender but still slightly crisp.

- Divide among warm bowls, scatter the cashews over and serve.

Note *Vegetarian oyster sauce is sometimes labelled mushroom sauce.*

Mains

THAI PINEAPPLE AND TOFU FRIED RICE

preparation time 25 minutes
cooking time 10 minutes
serves 4

1 small ripe pineapple

1 tablespoon peanut oil

150 g (5½ oz) snake (yard long) beans, cut into 5 cm (2 inch) lengths

4 red Asian shallots, finely chopped

4 garlic cloves, finely chopped

2 teaspoons grated fresh ginger

300 g (10½ oz/1½ cups) long-grain white rice, cooked

125 ml (4 fl oz/½ cup) vegetable stock

1 small carrot, coarsely grated

4 tofu puffs, cut into 1 cm (½ inch) cubes

3 spring onions (scallions), thinly sliced on the diagonal

2 tablespoons soy sauce

50 g (2 oz/⅓ cup) chopped roasted cashew nuts

1 small handful coriander (cilantro) leaves

2 long red chillies, seeded and thinly sliced

- Cut the skin off the pineapple and remove any eyes. Remove the core, then cut the pineapple into 1 cm (½ inch) cubes. Set aside.

- Heat the oil in a wok or frying pan over medium–high heat, swirling to coat the side. Add the snake beans and cook for 1–2 minutes, then add the shallot, garlic and ginger and stir-fry for 1 minute.

- Add the cooked rice and stock and stir-fry for 3 minutes, or until the rice is heated through. Add the pineapple, carrot, tofu and spring onion and stir-fry for 3 minutes. Add the soy sauce and toss to combine.

- Divide the fried rice among serving bowls and serve sprinkled with the cashews, coriander and chilli.

Mains

KUNG PAO WITH BROCCOLI AND PEANUTS

preparation time 15 minutes
cooking time 25 minutes
serves 4

270 g (9½ oz/1⅓ cups) long-grain
   white rice
2½ tablespoons peanut oil
4 garlic cloves, very thinly sliced
1½ tablespoons thinly sliced fresh
   ginger
2 long red chillies, thinly sliced on the
   diagonal
3 teaspoons sichuan peppercorns
600 g (1 lb 5 oz) broccoli, cut into
   florets, the larger ones cut in half
200 g (7 oz) mixed Asian mushrooms,
   such as enoki and shiitake,
   trimmed, and any large ones cut in
   half

2 tablespoons light soy sauce
3 teaspoons Chinese black rice
   vinegar
3 teaspoons caster (superfine) sugar
1½ teaspoons sesame oil
270 g (9½ oz) tin sliced water
   chestnuts, drained
110 g (4 oz/⅔ cup) roasted
   unsalted peanuts
4 spring onions (scallions), cut into
   4 cm (1½ inch) lengths

• Place the rice in a saucepan with 500 ml (17 fl oz/2 cups) water. Cover and bring to the boil, then immediately turn the heat down very low and simmer gently for 12 minutes, or until tender. Remove from the heat. Keeping the lid on, leave the rice to stand for 10 minutes.

• While the rice is standing, heat a wok over high heat. Add the peanut oil and swirl to coat the side. Add the garlic, ginger, chilli and peppercorns and stir-fry for 30 seconds, or until aromatic, being careful not to burn the garlic or it will become rancid..

- Add the broccoli and stir-fry for 2 minutes, then add the mushrooms and stir-fry for 1–2 minutes, or until the mushrooms are tender.

- Add the soy sauce, vinegar, sugar, sesame oil and water chestnuts. Toss until well combined and heated through.

- Finally add the peanuts and spring onion and stir for 30 seconds, or until the spring onion has just turned bright green, but has not collapsed.

- Serve immediately, with the steamed rice.

PAD SEE HEW

preparation time 20 minutes
cooking time 15 minutes
serves 4–6

80 ml (2½ fl oz/⅓ cup) kecap manis

2 tablespoons light soy sauce

1 tablespoon sambal oelek

1 tablespoon sugar

60 ml (2 fl oz/¼ cup) peanut oil

3 eggs, lightly beaten

100 g (3½ oz) tempeh, cut into thin strips, approximately 5 mm x 3 cm (¼ x 1¼ inches)

3 garlic cloves, finely chopped

2 bunches (about 750 g/1 lb 10 oz each) Chinese broccoli (gai larn), tough stem ends discarded, leaves coarsely shredded

450 g (1 lb) fresh flat rice noodles, separated

1–2 red bird's eye chillies, thinly sliced on the diagonal

50 g (2 oz/⅓ cup) roasted peanuts, coarsely chopped

lime wedges, to serve

● In a small bowl, mix together the kecap manis, soy sauce, sambal oelek and sugar. Set aside. In a large wok, heat 1 tablespoon of the oil over high heat and swirl to coat the side. Add the eggs and cook for about 1 minute, pushing the outside cooked areas into the centre as they cook. When the egg has set, transfer the omelette to a cutting board and cut into 1 cm (½ inch)-wide strips. Set aside.

● Heat the remaining oil in the wok. Add the tempeh and stir-fry for 2–3 minutes, or until just golden. Remove with a slotted spoon and drain on paper towels. Stir-fry the garlic in the wok for 30 seconds. Add the broccoli and cook, tossing the wok, for 2–3 minutes. Add the noodles and kecap manis mixture and stir-fry for a further 2–3 minutes. Add the tempeh and omelette strips and toss to combine and heat through. Divide the noodle mixture among serving bowls. Sprinkle with the chilli and peanuts and serve with lime wedges.

Mains

Index

Index

Index

Index